Studies in Judaism

THINGS UNUTTERABLE

Paul's Ascent to Paradise
in its Greco-Roman, Judaic, and
Early Christian Contexts

James D. Tabor

UNIVERSITY
PRESS OF
AMERICA

LANHAM • NEW YORK • LONDON

Copyright © 1986 by

University Press of America,® Inc.

4720 Boston Way
Lanham, MD 20706

3 Henrietta Street
London WC2E 8LU England

Library of Congress Cataloging in Publication Data

Tabor, James D., 1946-
  Things unutterable.

  (Studies in Judaism)
  Based on the author's thesis (Ph.D.)—University of
Chicago, 1981.
  Bibliography: p.
  Includes index.
  1. Bible.   N.T.   Corinthians, 2nd, XII, 2-4—
Criticism, interpretation, etc.   2. Paul, the Apostle,
Saint.   3. Ascension of the soul—History of doctrines—
Early church, ca. 30-600.   4. Voyages to the otherworld
—History of doctrines—Early church, ca. 30-600.
5. Rome—Religion. I. Title.   II. Series.
BS2675.2.T33   1986   225.9'24   86-18924
ISBN 0-8191-5643-4 (alk. paper)
ISBN 0-8191-5644-2 (pbk. : alk. paper)

THINGS UNUTTERABLE

**Paul's Ascent to Paradise
in its Greco-Roman, Judaic, and
Early Christian Contexts**

In loving memory of my Father
Elgie Lincoln Tabor
1911-1982

Table of Contents

PREFACE

The motif of the "heavenly journey" is familiar to all who study the ancient Mediterranean world. Yet it is the apostle Paul, leader in the early Christian movement, who provides us with a rare autobiographical account of such an ecstatic experience. He only offers us two short sentences, both tantalizingly cryptic, but they can provide an entrance into the ancient Jewish, early Christian, and Greco-Roman contexts in which such claims were made and maintained. The text presupposes that world of magic and mysticism, apocalyptic hopes, multiple realms of heaven populated with angels and demons, and reports of visions and revelations. In 1976, while at the University of Chicago, I chose this text, with its implications for understanding Paul's religious system, as my dissertation topic. This book developed out of that project. It is a broad study of Paul's thought and religious experience set in its wider Jewish/Greco-Roman contexts.

I would like to thank Robert M. Grant and Jonathan Z. Smith, both of the University of Chicago, who first introduced me to the study of religions of the ancient Mediterranean world. I came to the university at a fortunate time, since both of them taught in the Department of New Testament and Early Christian Literature. Each of them gave more to me than I could ever express. Also I express my gratitude to Jorunn Jacobsen Buckley, Eugene Gallagher, Naomi Janowitz, Patricia Cox Miller, and Bruce Woll, all fellow students at Chicago in the 1970's, and participants in our informal "ancient Mediterranean religions" seminar which met with Jonathan Z. Smith in those days. Each of them has contributed to my work in various ways through hours of discussion, helpful criticisms, and reading of drafts along the way. I also thank David Wilmont who helped me with Hebrew texts during that period. Robert Wilken and Joseph Blenkinsopp, with whom I taught and worked at the University of Notre Dame from 1979-85, continue to influence my work: one from the standpoint of the Patristic fathers and the culture of late antiquity; the other from the Hebrew Bible and Second Temple Judaism. I am particularly grateful to Morton Smith of Columbia University who patiently went through my manuscript and offered me many suggestions for revision. I appreciate the encouragement which Jacob Neusner, the editor of this series, continually gives to beginning scholars to put their work into print. Finally, I thank J. Andrew Foster, one of my students, who just graduated from William and Mary, for his help with editing and proofreading in the warm Williamsburg summer of 1986. As will be obvious to all who know the field, I have especially profited from the every stimulating, though often maligned, work on Paul done by Richard Reitzenstein and Albert Schweitzer in the 1920's. I hope this study will demonstrate how they complement one another. Reitzenstein never forgot Paul's basic affinity with other religions of "mystery" and "gnosis" in the Hellenistic period, while Schweitzer was willing to place him uncompromisingly in his apocalyptic setting. We now know that both were correct, in that the Judaism (or "Judaisms") of Paul's time was fully a part of that process we generally refer to as "hellenization," with apocalypticism being another manifestation of that very phenomenon.

Most of all I am grateful to my family, all along the way, for sacrificing time with me, each helping in his or her own ways, and especially to my father, who would have loved to have seen this final printed version of a project which he avidly followed and encouraged.

June, 1986
Williamsburg, Va.

CHAPTER ONE

INTRODUCTION

One of the more intriguing passages in the letters of Paul is his report of being caught up to heaven in 2 Cor. 12:2-4:[1]

> I know a man in Christ who fourteen years ago--whether in the body or out of the body I do not know, God knows--was caught up to the third heaven. And I know that this man--whether in the body or separate from the body I do not know, God knows--was caught up into Paradise and he heard unutterable words which are unlawful to speak.[2]

Here we have a precious bit of evidence of an actual *experience* of ascent to heaven from the early Roman imperial period. I emphasize the element of experience, because Paul's text is the only *firsthand* account of such a journey to heaven surviving from this period.[3] The passage also raises a series of questions for Pauline studies. What might such an experience have entailed? Why does he report it in this particular context? What relationship did it have to his gospel message or to his understanding of his apostolic authority and mission? Elsewhere, Paul claims to speak in ecstatic languages, to have "seen" the resurrected Jesus, and to have received his gospel through a personal "revelation" from Jesus.[4] How is this journey to heaven related to these other extraordinary experiences?

In surveying the history of interpretation one may distinguish three approaches to the passage: that of the early patristic fathers, the *religions-geschichtliche Schule*, and contemporary New Testament scholarship.

The early church fathers invariably treated the account as an objective, straightforward report of a highly privileged revelation given to Paul. Their interest was in the report per se, divorced from the context of Paul's battle with opponents at Corinth. The focus was on Paul's hearing of "things unutterable," and the disputed interpretations of that phrase. Clement of Alexandria cites the passage to support his argument for the ineffability of God:

> The apostle provides us with further evidence when he says, "I know a man in Christ caught up into the third heaven" and there "to paradise, who heard ineffable words which man has no power to speak." This is how he indicates the ineffability of

1

God when he uses the words "no power" he is not referring to any prohibition or fear of disobeying some command but is declaring that it is not within human capacity to express the divine, even though such expression may begin to be possible beyond the third heaven on the part of those whose function is the instruction of elect souls in the higher mysteries there.[5]

Irenaeus alludes to the passage in his discussion of whether God can preserve the bodies of the faithful. After citing the Hebrew Bible accounts of Enoch and Elijah, he writes:

Therefore the elders, as disciples of the apostles, relate to us that those translated were taken to that place, that same place where Paul was caught up and heard words that are unutterable for us in our present state. There those who have been translated will remain until the consummation, as a foretaste of immortality.[6]

More often the account comes up as a matter of dispute with various Gnostic groups who claimed that the authority for their doctrines was based on secrets revealed to Paul in heaven, which he subsequently passed on to a select few. Hippolytus says that the Naassenes made such a claim and he records a reference of Basilides to the phrase "ineffable words" in describing the mysteries of the heavenly world (*Refutation* 5. 8. 25; 7. 26. 7). Epiphanius, in discussing the sect of the Cainites, reports:

Again they falsify another little book in the name of Paul the apostle, full of things unspeakable, which the so-called Gnostics use, which they call the *Ascent of Paul*; the pretext [for so calling it] they find in the fact that the apostle says he ascended into the third heaven and heard ineffable words, which it is not permissible for a man to speak. And these, they claim, are the ineffable words.[7]

That various groups composed and used such books, which put an account of heavenly secrets into Paul's mouth, is beyond doubt. We have several editions of an *Apocalypse of Paul* from the fourth or fifth century, there are references to other similar texts, and Codex V of the Nag Hammadi library contains a Coptic work of the same title.[8] Tertullian argues against such a claim to secret revelation in his work *On Prescription of Heretics* 24:

Now, even though Paul was taken to the third heaven and was caught up to Paradise to hear certain revelations, this in no way implies that he taught another doctrine since the very nature of this revelation was that it could not be communicated to human beings.[9]

Irenaeus uses the passage to argue against those who claim to ascend above the realm of the Demiurge-Creater, whom they assert has only a material (animal), not a spiritual, nature:

> For that there are spiritual beings in the heavens is loudly proclaimed in all the scriptures. Paul testifies to this when he says he was caught up into the third heaven, and further, carried up to Paradise where he heard unutterable words which are unlawful to speak. What would that have profited him--to enter Paradise or the third heaven--if all these are under the realm of the Demiurge, yet, as some would hold, he was a participant in those mysteries which they say are above the Demiurge?

He goes on to make a further point:

> But since he reports his assumption to the third heaven as something exalted and privileged it is impossible that these are able to ascend above the seventh heaven since they are certainly not greater than the apostle.[10]

The early fathers, then, took the ascent report at face value, as a text from which they could argue various polemical points about the nature of the heavenly world. I know of no writer in this period who deals with it in its context in 2 Corinthians, or who explores its relationship to aspects of Paul's theology.

In modern times a very different approach has been taken by scholars of the *religionsgeschichtliche Schule*. The passage was often pointed to in stressing Paul's similarity to various forms of Oriental-Hellenistic spirituality and mysticism. Richard Reitzenstein's treatment of "Paulus als Pneumatiker" is perhaps the best example of this approach.[11] He repeatedly refers to the ascent account as evidence for understanding Paul as an adept and formulator of a Hellenistic gnostic mystery religion.[12] In his opening programmatic lecture he concludes:

> We encounter in him [Paul] the beginnings of that basic Hellenistic consciousness, and the religio-historical way of considering these matters may place him in this course of development not as the first, but perhaps as the greatest of all the gnostics.[13]

For Reitzenstein, the key to Pauline theology is his understanding of *gnōsis*, which involves the nonmediated vision of God-- what he calls the "Hellenistic mystery."[14] Such *gnōsis* is given by heavenly revelation, bringing both enlightenment and authority:[15]

> Alongside the appeal to an original revelation and tradition there stands, as a second source of faith, a steadily ongoing direct revelation of the deity to his servants. The climactic

3

> point of the religious life is formed by the ecstasy which reaches its fullest and most unerring form in the mystery. When man is united with God in mystery, he must thereby attain a direct, nonmediated knowledge that is independent of all earlier knowledge, and from this time on, God speaks through the servant who is consecrated to him; thus for the believer this new message stands alongside the earlier one with equal validity or even above it.[16]

He sees the ascent experience as the "highest vision" to which Paul appeals, even surpassing the miracle of his conversion.[17] Although his major treatment of the text does include a brief exegetical consideration of the context of 2 Cor. 10-13, his main purpose is to demonstrate how the central features of Paul's religious experience and thought are paralleled in a wide range of texts from the Hellenistic period. This history-of-religions approach to Paul has had considerable influence, spawning a series of studies debating the question of Paul's relationship to the so-called "mystery religions," and whether or to what extent he can be regarded as a "mystic."[18] The report of Paul's ascent to Paradise is often brought into such discussions. This focus on Paul's religious *experience* as well as his theological ideas, has considerably advanced Pauline studies.

Many recent treatments of the ascent passage by New Testament scholars reflect neither the concerns or the views of the fathers, nor the history-of-religions school. It has generally been argued that Paul disparaged such ecstatic experiences and that his journey to heaven had little or no connection with his message or his claim of apostolic authority.[19] This line of argument is based on an exegesis of 2 Cor. 10-13 which attempts to set Paul against the opponents at Corinth, claiming that his theology of the cross, and his emphasis on suffering, run contrary to any cultivation of ecstatic experiences of revelation. Although the question must be argued on its own merits, and with careful consideration of the way Paul reports his experience in the 2 Corinthian context, this approach to the text by many New Testament scholars seems to have a hidden agenda. The early fathers had no problem with taking Paul at face value. As Daniélou has made so clear, they shared his mythological-magical cosmos in which journeys to heaven made perfect sense.[20] Indeed, this is the common "background" of the Greco-Roman period.[21] Reitzenstein and others accepted the implications of this to the fullest extent. That Paul even reports such an experience places him completely in this world, not as a bystander, somehow strangely "modern," but as a full participant. Those who want to separate Paul from this world of magic and mysticism, either chronologically or theologically, operate with what Robert Wilken called, in another context, a "Eusebian" view of the past.[22] It is assumed, because Paul is Paul (i.e., great Christian theologian and apostle), he is somehow "pure" of the magical-mystical elements associated with ascent to heaven in other materials of the period (especially the Greek magical papyri, or something like *Sepher HaRazim*)[23] Jacob Neusner has repeatedly documented similar attempts to mark off periods or figures or

4

sources belonging to a "pure" past (conceived in various ways) by scholars working in the area of Judaism in late antiquity.[24] This essentially "fundamentalist" tendency is encountered often in the history of the "history" of religions.

Obviously, the account must be interpreted in its context, but at the same time be taken seriously for what it is, a first-hand report of Paul's religious experience. This broader religious context, in which reports of heavenly journeys were frequent and important, must be taken into account as well. Finally, it must be evaluated in the light of Paul's message and his claim to be an apostle.

In the next chapter I shall begin with a consideration of that message and his understanding of his apostolic authority and mission. Paul's "gospel" involved a vision of the end of history and a cosmic triumph, which, like his ascent, must be seen in its Hellenistic context.[25] He understood his own role in that apocalyptic plan of God to be a crucial one. In chapter three I shall move outside the Pauline corpus to survey the motif of the heavenly journey in antiquity. There I am interested in how the idea of ascent to heaven was variously understood and how such conceptions were related to the more concrete questions of religious and cultic experience. In my final chapter I shall examine the text itself, bringing in the results of the previous two chapters and drawing my conclusions.

Besides these general parameters, my work will be limited to the six letters of unquestioned authenticity.[26] The perennial "Hellenistic vs. Judaic" debate will not appear, since I am convinced that emerging Christianity and the other forms of Second Temple Judaism *are*, by definition, "Hellenistic" (strictly, Roman imperial) religions, essentially similar to the other religions of the period.[27] Certainly Paul's background is "Jewish." Still, this does not mean that the work of scholars such as Reitzenstein or Bousset is flawed in bringing into the discussion non-Jewish materials. It is a reductionistic view of Judaism which has to speak of "borrowings" whenever a so-called "Hellenistic" emphasis or motif is encountered. Consequently, my intention is neither to *explain* Paul from some notion of "background" (moving from "parallels" to "influences" to "sources") nor to try to somehow prove his uniqueness.[28] No two texts, two figures, or two religions of the period are the same. Given the fragmentary nature of our evidence it is rare to find clear indications of historical links, influences, or direct connections. Even with a collection of related materials such as the New Testament or the *Corpus Hermeticum*, it is difficult enough to posit theories of influence. My interest is in certain structural similarities and differences discernible in texts which contain the idea of the heavenly journey, as clues to issues and questions which might otherwise be overlooked. Finally, I am acutely aware that the results of this study are in the end largely theoretical. Paul's strangeness from ourselves must never be forgotten as we seek to understand his ideas, religious experience, or cultic practice. Only seven letters are indisputably from his hand, all written within the decade of the 50's C.E. We know little more about him or the communities he addressed. It is difficult to read these texts without hearing 1900 years of theological argument and commentary in the background. In one sense we are *too* familiar with these texts; we know too much. Perhaps this very account of his ecstatic ascent, more than any other bit of evidence, serves to remind us of our distance.

NOTES TO CHAPTER ONE

1. Despite the use of the third person, I think it is clear that Paul is speaking of his own experience. The chronological note in 12:2 and the first person reference in 12:7 makes this obvious.

2. Translations of ancient texts and emphases therein are my own throughout this book unless otherwise indicated.

3. In chapter 3 I will survey the texts from this period which speak of ascent to heaven. Although we have many references to such journeys as well as pseudonymous accounts of such, Paul's text is a rarity in that it is autobiographical.

4. 1 Cor. 14:8 (cf. 13:1); 9:1 and 15:8; Gal 1:11-12. These passages will be discussed in the following chapter.

5. *Miscellanies* 5. 12. 79. See *The Instructor* 37 for a further reference by Clement to the passage. It should be noted that Clement, like most patristic fathers, seems to see the passage as reporting either two separate journeys or one journey in two stages. Compare the accounts of Irenaeus and Tertullian below.

6. *Against Heresies* 5. 5. 1.

7. *Against Heresies* 38. 2. 5.

8. See *NTA*, 1:755-803, for a translation of and introduction to the *Apocalypse of Paul*. For the Nag Hammadi text see James M. Robinson, ed., *The Nag Hammadi Library* (New York: Harper & Row, 1977), pp. 239-41.

9. Compare *Scorpiace* 12 for a similar use of the Pauline passage. In a different context he alludes to Paul's ascent in his work *Against Marcion* 1. 15; 5. 12.

10. *Against Heresies* 2. 30. 7-8.

11. Chap. 16 of his book *Hellenistic Mystery-Religions: Their Basic Ideas and*

INTRODUCTION

Significance (Pittsburgh: Pickwick Press, 1978), pp. 426-500. Generally I have in mind the work of Wilhelm Bousset, Martin Dibelius, Wilhelm Heitmüller, Albrecht Dieterich and Hans Windisch.

12. *Hellenistic Mystery-Religions*, pp. 82-84, 86-87, 459-84.

13. Ibid., p. 84

14. Ibid., p. 3-107.

15. This idea of enlightenment is drawn from Paul's use of words such as *gnōsis, photizein, doxazein,* and *metamorphousthai,* see pp. 426-59.

16. Ibid., p. 32. Reitzenstein makes extensive use of Apuleius' account of Lucius' call, conversion and initiation (*Metamorphoses* 11), pp. 274-92, 38-46.

17. Ibid., pp. 82, 469.

18. Some of the major studies are: Gustav Anrich, *Das antike Mysterienwesen in seinem Einfluss auf das Christentum* (Gottingen, n.p., 1894); H. A. A. Kennedy, *St. Paul and the Mystery Religions* (London: Hodder & Stoughton, 1913); Kurt Deissner, *Paulus und die Mystik seiner Zeit,* 2d ed. (Leipzig: A. Deichert'sche Verlagsbuchhandlung,1921); Alfred Wilkenhauser, *Pauline Mysticism* (New York: Herder & Herder, 1960); Arthur Darby Nock, *Early Gentile Christianity and Its Hellenistic Background* (New York: Harper & Row, Harper Torchbooks, 1964); Gunter Wagner, *Pauline Baptism and the Pagan Mysteries* (Edinburgh: Oliver & Boyd, 1967).

19. One of the most recent examples is William Baird, "Visions, Revelation, and Ministry: Reflections on 2 Cor 12:1-5 and Gal 1:11-17," *JBL* 104 (1985): 651-662. I will survey some of the major studies in the following chapters.

20. See Jean Daniélou, *The Theology of Jewish Christianity* (Chicago: Henry Regnery, 1964), passim, and *Gospel Message and Hellenistic Culture* (Philadelphia: Westminster Press, 1973), especially pp. 427-506.

21. See the fine summary description by Morton Smith in *Jesus the Magician* (New York: Harper & Row, 1978), pp. 4-5, as well as his extensive description of "The Background" (Chapter 4) in *Clement of Alexandria and a Secret Gospel of Mark* (Cambridge: Harvard University Press, 1973), pp. 195-278.

22. See his *Myth of Christian Beginnings* (Notre Dame: University of Notre Dame Press, 1980), passim.

23. Wesley Carr's study *Angels and Principalites* (Cambridge: Cambridge University Press, 1981) is a perfect example of this attempt to place the "crazy " stuff after Paul.

24. See his "Methodology in Talmudic History" printed in *Ancient Judaism: Debates and Disputes* (Missoula: Scholars Press, 1984), pp. 5-24; as well as his reviews of Urbach and others, pp. 79-141; and his reviews of Goodenough's *Jewish Symbols*, pp. 145-180. He points out how the most basic work of scholars such as Morton Smith and E. R. Goodenough is largely ignored by many who try to do "Jewish history."

25. I presented the briefest outline of this in "Paul's Notion of 'Many Sons of God' and its Hellenistic Contexts," *Helios* 13 (1986): 87-97.

26. 1 Thess., 1 and 2 Cor., Rom., Gal., Phil. I have not had occasion to use Philemon in this study.

27. The debate is both summarized and reflected in the second chapter of Albert Schweitzer's book, *The Mysticism of Paul the Apostle* (London: Adam & Charles Black, 1953), pp. 26-40, which he titles "Hellenistic or Judaic?" The story (still apparently untold to many) of how this dichotomy has been gradually broken down would take pages to document. Morton Smith's article, "The Image of God," *BJRL* 40 (1958): 473-512 is a good start; also the general article of Jonathan Smith, "Hellenistic Religions," *Encyclopedia Britannica: Macropedia*, 8: 749-51, and Neusner's reviews of Goodenough (note 24 above) provide a helpful orientation.

28. See Samuel Sandmel's interesting observations, "Parallelomania," *JBL* 81 (1962): 1-13.

CHAPTER TWO

PAUL'S MESSAGE AND MISSION

In this chapter I wish to investigate two areas of Paul's thought, each of which will serve as a basis for evaluating the significance of his experience of ascent to Paradise: first, his message, then his understanding of his apostolic authority and mission.

The Message

Much of the debate among Pauline scholars in this century has been over the question of the center of Paul's theology.[1] E. P. Sanders has provided one of the more persuasive presentations of the case that Paul's central ideas develop from his experience of being "in Christ" and vice versa (what he calls "participatory" in contrast to "juristic").[2] With Sanders' treatment of Paul's understanding of the Law, righteousness by faith, the human plight, et al., I basically agree, as I do with his notion that we should ask how a religious system *as a whole* and on its own terms "worked." However, his description of how a religion is perceived by its adherents to function as "how getting in and staying in are understood," does not lead one to consider *why* they wanted in in the first place: Paul's converts wanted *salvation*, and yet this is something that Paul rarely stops to define.[3] This salvation involved more than a particular understanding of God's grace and forgiveness of sins.[4] Sanders' statement that Paul's primary conviction is that "Jesus Christ is Lord, that in him God has provided for the salvation of all those who believe . . . , and that he will soon return to bring all things to an end," is a good general summary, but needs to be more fully laid out.[5] Paul's understanding of salvation involves a rather astounding (at least to modern ears) scheme of "mass apotheosis" and imminent cosmic takeover. We must turn to the essential passages which more fully treat the *content* of this salvation which Paul offered his followers.

Firstborn of Many Brothers

In Rom. 8:29-30 Paul provides a sequential outline of what he calls the *plan* (*prothesis*--v. 28)[6] of God for all his converts. I shall present a rather tight and technical analysis of his language here, and how it connects to his discussions elsewhere. I want to show that he is at least coherent, if not systematic, when it come to what I believe is central to his whole salvation message: his belief that a new cosmic family--immortal "Sons of God" he calls them--is soon to be dramatically revealed as an agent for carrying forth the final stages of God's plan for his creation. He sketches the essentials in a few lines:

> For those whom he foreknew (*proegnō*) he also predestined (*proōrisen*) to share the image (*summorphous tēs eikonos*) of his Son, that he might be the *firstborn of many brothers*, and the ones he predestined he also called (*ekalesen*), and the ones he called he also justified, and the ones he justified he also glorified (*edoxasen*).

These carefully composed verses function as a theological climax to this section of the letter. They come at the end of Paul's sustained presentation of his gospel message in 1:16-8:25, thus offering an epitome of Paul's system of belief. The central elements break down into three groupings.

1. The Predetermined Secret Plan
    The first two thought units are expressed by the verbs "to foreknow" and "to predestine." "To foreknow" (*proginōskō*) is used only one other time by Paul, in Rom. 11:2, where he refers to the selection of the nation of Israel. In both passages its object is the group, or people, of God, *for whom* the purpose of God is to be unfolded. He uses "to predestine" (*proorizō*) in only one other place as well, 1 Cor. 2:7, where it is also closely connected to this same idea of a secret "plan" of God:

> But we impart a secret and hidden wisdom of God, which God determined (*proōrisen*)before the ages *for our glorification*.

Here, as in Rom. 8:29, "to predestine" or "to determine" is directly connected to the idea of glorification (*doxa*), even though the vocabulary and context of this section of 1 Corinthians is quite different from that of Romans.[7] This concept of *doxa* can consistently epitomize God's ultimate goal, although Paul is addressing desperate situations in his letters. The prefix *pro-*, in both verbs of Rom 8:29, indicates priority in relation to the next mentioned action, i.e. first knowledge, then designation, (then calling, followed by justification, and finally glorification). However, the phrase "before the ages" (*pro tōn aiōnōn*), would indicate that in Paul's thinking the original formulation of this plan of God took place before "the present evil age" (Gal. 1:4).[8] It should also be noted that in 1 Cor. 2:7 Paul says he teaches or speaks "in secret," or perhaps "in a mystery" (*en mustērion*). Later he writes of the transformation or *glorification* of believers which is to take place at the return of Christ from heaven (1 Cor. 15:51), and he calls it a "secret" or "mystery."[9] This secret plan, hidden from the "rulers of this age" (*archontōn*--which I take to be a reference to hostile spirits in the heavenly realms who exercise powers of fate and death--1 Cor 2:8),[10] relates ultimately to glorification. Both to "foreknow" and "to predestine" in Rom 8:29 should be understood in this cosmological sense. The point is not only that God has known and determined something beforehand, but that salvation for the select group is a strategy on God's part in a hostile cosmological context. This is obviously what he has in mind in the following verses of the chapter (31-39), where he lists the various spiritual powers of the heavens who will be conquered by Christ.

2. A Cosmic Family

The phrases (1) "to share the image of his Son" and (2) "that he might be the firstborn of many brothers," indicate (1) the immediate content of God's decree; and (2) one of its consequences.

Since Paul thought sharing the form of Christ involved sharing his death (2 Cor. 4:10), sharing the form cannot be immediately equated with glorification (i.e., it stands here at the beginning of the list of stages that concludes with glorification). The word used here in the phrase " sharing the image" (*summorphos*) occurs elsewhere only in Phil. 3:21, where Paul has this identical sequence in mind, but is referring to the final stage, the glorification or transformation of the believer at the heavenly return of Jesus. He writes:

> For our commonwealth exists in the heavens, from which we expect a Savior, the Lord Jesus Christ, who will *transform* our lowly body into the same form (*summorphon*) as his *glorious* body, by the power with which he is able to subject everything to himself.[11]

A related verbal form of *summorphos*: *metamorphoomai*; is used in 2 Cor. 3:18, along with *eikōn* ("form" or "image"), which is the other key term in the phrase ("sharing the image") from Rom. 8:29.

> But we all, with unveiled face, beholding the glory of the Lord, are being transformed (*metamorphoumetha*)into his image (*eikona*) from one degree of glory to another; for this comes from the Lord who is the Spirit.

Although the meaning and context of this verse is difficult,[12] I do not think one finds here, or in the following section of 2 Cor. 5:1-10, any shift from the idea that transformation/glorification is completed only at the return of Jesus from heaven.[13] Even though he uses the present tense in 2 Cor. 3:18, coupled with the phrase "from one degree of glory to another," (*apo doxēs eis doxan*), the thought is the same as Rom. 8:29. It is his use of *eikōn* ("image") which I find striking. Phil. 3:21 shows that he has in mind a transformation of what he calls the *sōma* ("body"). He elaborates his idea of a transformed body in 1 Cor. 15, which I will discuss below. This connection of *eikōn* with *doxa* occurs elsewhere. In 2 Cor. 4:4 he speaks of the god of this age who has blinded the eyes of unbelievers so that they can not see the "light of the gospel of the glory (*tēs doxēs*) of Christ, who is in the image (*eikōn*) of God." In verse 6 he says that God's illumination of the hearts of these believers

11

brings about the "light of the knowledge of the glory (*tēs doxēs*) of God in the face of Christ." Paul's message is a gospel *of* the glory of Christ, i.e., a *gnōsis* of the glory of God seen in Christ, who is the *eikōn* of God.[14] Such language is not mere rodomontade. We are dealing here with the heart of Paul's system of thought, the belief that Christ bears the image and glory of God, and that believers in Christ have already begun to share the *glory* of Christ, being transformed into his *image*, and will share it completely in the End.

The second phrase, "that he might be the firstborn of many brothers," stands as an expansion of the thought about sharing the image of God. The word translated "first-born" (*prōtotokos*) occurs only here in Paul.[15] The idea is closely linked to Paul's argument in 1 Cor. 15 (vv. 20-28; 42-58) where the term *aparchē* ("first fruits") is used as a basis for arguing that Jesus' transformation or glorification foreshadows that of the many "in Christ" who follow. "First-born" as used here is therefore anticipatory, pointing toward recapitulation. It means more than preeminence; it implies there are those who will be "later-born." The equation of Jesus the Son of God, with the *many* glorified sons of God to follow is God's means of bringing into existence a *family* (i.e., "many brothers") of cosmic beings, the *Sons of God*, who share his heavenly *doxa*. Or, to put it another way, Jesus already stands at the head of a new *genus* of cosmic "brothers" who await their full transformation at his arrival from heaven. Paul uses the verb *doxazō* ("to glorify") to indicate the conclusion to which both these phrases of Rom. 8:29 point, summarizing the idea of the "hope of sharing the glory of God" which he introduced in Rom. 5:1 and develops in 8:17-25. To be a "son of God" (or "child of God," which is his other phrase in this chapter) through receiving the Holy Spirit (Rom. 8:14-16), is to be an *heir*, even a *co-heir* with Jesus. Such a relationship involves a suffering with him (8:17), along with glorification (*sundoxazō*) like his, but the suffering will be transient, the glory will endure. Paul uses the various forms of the word "heir" (*klēronomos*) frequently.[16] That the concept is connected to complete glorification at the return of Jesus from heaven is clear, not only in Rom. 8:17, but by comparing 1 Cor. 6:9-10; 15:50-53; Gal. 5:21; Phil. 3:20-21 and 1 Thess. 2:12. One inherits the "kingdom of God" *at* the return of Jesus and *through* a transformation to immortal heavenly life. Paul's discussion of the validity of the Torah, of how one is declared righteous, and of whether Gentiles must become 'Jews' to be a part of God's elect people has to do with the issue of *who* is to be considered an *heir*. The *klēronomia* is not from the Torah (Gal. 3:18; 4:30; Rom. 4:14). It belongs to those who are "sons of God" by faith in the Christ, stemming from the promise made to Abraham that he would "inherit the world [cosmos]" (Rom. 4:13; Gal. 3:26-29; 4:1-7). Thus, Paul's whole treatment of the Law in Rom. 1:16-4:25 and Gal. 3-4 must be seen as *subsidiary* to a broader concept, the meaning and content of the *klēronomia*. For Paul this concept moves far beyond the idea of inheriting the land of Israel, or hopes of national restoration. It is rulership over the entire *cosmos*. He exultantly writes:

> For I think that the sufferings of this present time are not worth comparing with the *glory that is about to be revealed in us*! (Rom. 8:18)

This is the climax toward which his presentation in Romans (beginning in 1:16) moves. He then proceeds to explain how this glory is to be revealed and what it will involve:

> For the creation expectantly longs for the *revealing of the Sons of God*; since it was subjected to futility, not through its own desire but by the will of the one who subjected it in hope; because the *creation itself will be set free from its enslavement to corruption* obtaining the freedom of the glory of the children of God. Because we know that the whole creation has been groaning in birth pangs until now; but not only the creation but we too, who have the first fruits of the Spirit, we groan inside waiting for our *sonship*, that is, the *redemption of our bodies*. For we were saved in this very hope. Now hope that is seen is not hope, for who hopes for what he sees? But if we hope for what we do not see we wait for it patiently. (Rom. 8:19-25)

Just as in Phil. 3:21, which I have already quoted, Paul has in mind here the transformation of the body, i.e., its release from decay and glorification at the return of Christ from heaven. The use of the word *huiothesia* (translated "sonship"--v 23) to refer to this event is significant. Several manuscripts (chiefly Western) omit the word, probably because it appears to contradict 8:15:[17]

> For you did not receive the spirit of bondage to fall back into fear, but you have received the spirit of *sonship* (*huiothesia*) in which we cry out "Abba! Father!"

In Gal. 4:4-7 Paul expresses the identical thought:

> But when the fullness of time arrived, God sent forth his Son, born of woman, born under the law, to redeem those who were under the law, so that we might receive *sonship* (*huiothesian*). And because you are sons, God has sent the Spirit of his Son into our hearts crying, "Abba! Father!" So through God you are no longer a slave but a son, and if a son then an *heir* (*klēronomos*).

I don't think there is any necessary contradiction here regarding the meaning of "sonship." Believers now receive the *spirit of sonship* and are sons of God and heirs with Christ (Rom. 8:17). Gal. 4:4-7 parallels this thought. The reason for the "sending of the Son" was that believers might receive this "sonship." The completion of the process is identified in Rom. 8:23 precisely as "the redemption [i.e., transformation] of the body" which comes at the return of Christ. This tension between present inception and future con-

13

summation is common in Paul.[18] I have already noted 2 Cor. 3:18, where he speaks of glorification as a process already begun (cf. 2 Cor. 4:7-12). In 2 Cor. 5:5 Paul refers to the Spirit as a "down payment" or "first installment" (*ton arrabōna*). Note also that Paul links the release of the *creation* itself to the the realization of the destiny of the Sons of God, a complicated notion with which he also deals in 1 Cor. 15:20-28. This underlines the *cosmic* aspect of Paul's understanding of final salvation.

3. The Implementation of the Secret Plan

This cosmic plan of bringing forth "many brothers" is implemented through God's "*calling*," "*justifying*," and "*glorifying*" the special group of believers (Rom. 8:30). This idea of calling (*kaleō*) occurs frequently in Paul's letters.[19] In 1 Thess. 2:12 he exhorts the group to "live a life worthy of God who *calls you* into his own *kingdom* and *glory*." Here again Paul connects the idea of inheriting the kingdom with that of glory. Those who are transformed from flesh and blood existence (i.e., glorified) at the coming of Christ from heaven are those who "inherit the kingdom of God" (1 Cor. 15:42-52). The one word "justify" here (*dikaioō*) summarizes the complexities of Paul's whole argument in Rom. 1:16-4:25 (i.e. "justification by faith") and represents as well the *results* of that justified life which he discusses in 5:1-8:17. Rom. 5:1-2 states the position of the community living in the time of the end:

> Therefore *being justified by faith* we have peace with God through our Lord Jesus Christ, through whom we have access to this grace in which we stand and we rejoice in the *hope of partaking of the glory of God*.

The combined sense of *kaleō* and *dikaioō* is that Paul's gospel message divides humanity into two distinct groups. There are those being saved and those perishing, those being reconciled to God and those yet his enemies, those being justified by faith and those under his wrath, those who have begun to see the light and those whom Satan has blinded (1 Cor. 1:18; 2 Cor. 2:14-16; 4:3-6; 18-21). God has called his elect ones and begun their justification, has made them Sons of God through the Spirit, and has destined them for the final glorification at the return of Jesus from heaven. It should be noted that all five of the main verbs in Rom. 8:29-30 (foreknow, predestine, call, justify, glorify) are in the aorist tense. In a single stroke Paul sketches out the key elements of his understanding of God's cosmic plan--the final glorification of many Sons of God.

The Last Adam

This teaching of Paul regarding the glorification of many Sons of God is obviously tied to his understanding of the glorification of Jesus and his status as firstborn "Son of God," exalted Lord of the cosmos. Paul sees in the career of Jesus the model of this plan involving the many to follow. He

14

understands Jesus to be a kind of second or last "Adam" who has shown the way for the whole race. In Phil. 2:6-11 Paul quotes an early Christian hymn which reflects this pattern of salvation:[20]

    a) He was in the *form* of God (*morphē theou*),
    b) but did not consider *equality* with God (*einai isa theǭ*) something to be *grasped*, but emptied himself,
    c) taking on the form of a slave.

    a) Being in the likeness of men,
    b) and found in human form, he *humbled himself*,
    c) becoming obedient to the point of death.
    [even death on a cross]

    a) Because of this God has *highly exalted* him,
    b) and given him a name,
    c) above every name.

    a) That at the name of Jesus
    b) every knee should bow in heaven, and on earth, and under the earth,
    c) And every tongue confess that Jesus is Lord, to the glory of God the father.

I have arranged the hymn in four stanzas of three lines each following the structure proposed by Charles Talbert (with the phrase "even death on a cross" excepted as a Pauline addition).[21] Stanzas one and two parallel one another. Rather than describing a move from divine heavenly life to mortal human, they both state in parallel fashion the choice made by this second Adam. I therefore cautiously agree with Talbert and others that the hymn is *not* presenting the notion of a pre-existent descending/ascending heavenly figure, but rather builds on a contrast developed from the story of Adam in Gen. 3. Here a second "Adam," who though *made in God's image* (Gen 1:26), does not *grasp at equality with God*, as the first Adam did when he took the forbidden fruit (Gen 3:5-6), but through humble obedience shows the true way to exaltation.[22] Paul is exhorting the community to have the same attitude of mind so that they too can experience a similar exaltation (Phil. 3:12-21).

It is in 1 Cor. 15 that Paul offers his most systematic treatment of the destiny of the elect as related to the career of Jesus as a second Adam. There was a party at Corinth which was saying that "there is no resurrection of the dead"(15:12). The position of those making such a denial is difficult, if not impossible to determine.[23] Some would take the denial as an expression of skepticism, perhaps akin to the position of the Epicureans or that of an ultraconservative Jewish group like the Sadducees, who denied the very idea of an afterlife.[24] A more common interpretation has been that we have here a "Platonizing" position which viewed the notion of the resurrection of the *body* as crude and superfluous.[25] The position favored by most scholars is that some were denying the futurity of the resurrection, claiming in some way to *already* be experiencing that mode of existence. It is conceivable that such a group might have denied both the somatic *and* future aspects of the resurrection doctrine. To further compound the problem, one must ask whether Paul himself clearly understood the position of this group.[26]

What has been overlooked too often is that while the occasion of Paul's discussion was some type of denial of the resurrection of the *dead*, the chapter as a whole deals not so much with resurrection (which for the community would apply only to the minority who had died, cf. 1 Thess. 4:13-18), as with transformation or change *of the living and the dead* at the return of Jesus from heaven. In other words, the lines of his discussion in 15:20-28 and 35-58 apply to those *alive* at the coming of Christ as much as to those of the group who have died. Thus Paul writes:

> I tell you this, brothers: *flesh and blood cannot inherit the kingdom of God*, neither does the perishable inherit the imperishable! Lo! I reveal to you a secret! We shall not all sleep [die], but we shall *all be changed* (*allagēsometha*), in a moment, in the twinkling of an eye, at the final trumpet. For the trumpet will sound and the dead will be raised imperishable and *we* [i.e., those living] *shall be changed* (vv. 50-52).

I would argue that, in this context at least, Paul's affirmation of the resurrection of the dead is essentially his way of affirming the *participation* of the "dead in Christ" in the final glorification (i.e., change of the dead/mortal body, Phil. 3:20-21; Rom. 8:18-24) which was expected at the return of Jesus. Paul does not elaborate on the "state of the dead," preferring the metaphor of sleep, but he is emphatic on the point that the change from mortal to immortal body is *at*, not before, the appearance of Jesus from heaven. There is an "order" (*tagma*) involved in this secret plan of God (v. 23). Paul declares that "all shall be made alive" (*zōopoieō*), but each in his own order (v. 23). It is clear that the verb "to make alive" refers to more than raising the bodies of the dead; it is equivalent to *allassō* ("to be changed") in verses 51-52 and includes the living as well.

The other problem, whether actually raised by some of the Corinthians, or anticipated by Paul (v. 35) was that of the "somatic" nature of this transformed immortal existence. Here, as in Phil. 3:21 (and implicitly in Rom. 8:23), Paul speaks of a glorified *body* (*sōma*). Specifically, he contrasts the mortal "flesh and blood" body which he labels *psuchikon* (here meaning "natural" or "physical"), with the "spiritual body" (*pneumatikon*) which is to come (v. 44b). He builds his case on what appears to be his own midrash on Gen. 2:7.[27]

> Thus it is written, "The first man Adam became a living being" [physical being], the last Adam became a life-giving spirit (v. 45).

16

His phrase, "life-giving spirit" (*pneuma zōopoioun*), is equivalent to his "spiritual body," and is related to his use of the same verb, "to make alive" in verse 23.

The implications of this Adam typology are striking: as Adam was the head of a race of physical human beings, subject to corruption and death; so Jesus (as a last Adam) is the first of a transformed race or *genus* of heavenly beings, immortal and glorified. That Jesus is *human* (i.e., mortal, "Adam") is crucial since his transformation to an immortal, glorious state is representative for all those who follow. Paul makes this clear in v. 21:

> For as by a *human* [Adam] death came, so by a *human* has come also the resurrection of the dead.

As we have seen, by the phrase "resurrection of the dead" here, Paul includes this whole cosmic reality: the transformation/glorification from mortal to immortal heavenly life. This pattern of salvation, seen here and in Phil. 2:5-10, is the same as Rom. 1:3-4, which most scholars take to be a pre-Pauline confession.[28] Paul describes the "gospel of God" as that:

> ... concerning his Son, who became a descendant of David according to the flesh and was appointed Son of God in power according to the Spirit of holiness from a resurrection of the dead, Jesus Christ our Lord.

Paul sets forth six contrasts in 1 Cor. 15 which describe what is involved in this "change" from a "First Adam" type of existence to that of "Last Adam":

1. "living physical being" to "life-giving spirit" (v. 45)

2. "perishable" to "imperishable" (v. 42)

3. "dishonor" to "glory" (v. 43)

4. "weakness" to "power" (v. 43)

5. "physical body" to "spiritual body" (v. 44)

6. "from the earth, of dust" to "of heaven" (v. 47)

At the end of this section he concludes:

> Just as we have borne the image of the one of dust, we shall also bear the image of the heavenly one (v. 49).

The terms which characterize the existence of "first Adam" apply *equally* to

17

the man Jesus as well as to all humankind, while those of "last Adam" apply *equally* to the exalted Christ as well as to the destiny of the select group.

The idea of "inheriting the kingdom," is closely connected to this notion of transformation, as I noted above (1 Cor. 15:50). In 1 Cor. 15:20-28 Paul presents an overview, which to us must necessarily remain cryptic, of the plan of God from the resurrection of Jesus (the "first fruits" of the harvest) until the *telos*, or final end, when God will be "all things to all" (v. 28). He evidently saw the time period between the return of Christ from heaven to transform the elect, *until* this final end, as one of cosmic battle and conquest of hostile demonic forces.[29] He speaks of Christ "destroying every rule, authority, and power," and finally death itself (vv. 24-26). He quotes Psa. 8:6 (which in turn is an interpretation of Gen. 1:26), which says that God has put "all things under his [mankind's] feet." He applies it, in keeping with his Adam typology, to *the man* Jesus Christ, but by extension to this whole new race of heavenly "Adams." Earlier he had reminded the Corinthians:

> Don't you know that the saints are going to judge the world (*kosmon*)? If the world is to be judged by you, are you incompetent to handle petty cases? Don't you know that we will *judge angels*? How much more matters pertaining to this life! (6:2-3).

He assures them that "all things" belong to them (3:21-23). This same theme of cosmic conquest is also found in Rom. 8:37-39. God has given Jesus the power to "subject all things to himself" and this *energeia* will be manifested at his return from heaven when he glorifies his chosen ones (Phil. 3:21). To inherit the kingdom or rule of God, then, is to share in this cosmic power and glory, or as he puts it in Rom. 8:17, to be a *co-inheritor* with Christ.

Robin Scroggs and others have argued from these texts that Paul understands the nature of Christ in his resurrected existence as a "human nature." He represents "true man" and thus opens the way for mankind to achieve the "true humanity" intended at the creation.[30] Although one finds some support for this in Paul's interpretation of Gen. 2:7 in 1 Cor. 15:45-49, one must not miss the radical implications of Paul's understanding of the destiny of the elect group. Paul develops his exegesis from Gen. 1:27 and Psa. 8:6 as well. These texts speak of man in the "image" (*eikōn*) of God, having "all things placed under his feet." Paul interprets this in the light of Christ, who is the "image of God" (Rom. 8:29; 2 Cor. 3:18) and has been given all rule and authority (1 Cor. 15:24; Phil. 2:10) with "all things" subject to him. So it takes on the vastly expanded meaning of *cosmic* rule, power, and exaltation. What is said of Jesus as glorified Son of God, is also said of those "many brothers" who follow.[31] In the wider context of Hellenistic religions, it makes little sense to speak of an exalted, heavenly, group of immortals, who are designated "Sons of God," as *human beings*. The old rubric, "Gods are immortal, humans are mortal" is apt here. Paul's understanding of salvation involves a particularly Jewish notion of *apotheosis*, and would have been understood as such by his converts.

Paul's message of salvation then is a message about cosmic conquest and liberation. The elect group are freed from their bondage to death and mortality brought on by sin. They are released from the power of Satan and his demonic forces which rule the cosmos. As glorified immortals they will participate with Christ, in the rule of God, bringing about the final end of all opposition to his will.

I would argue that this idea of heavenly *glorification* is the core of Paul's message. I have noted his use of the terms *doxa/doxazō* in various contexts to summarize his overall view of God's plan of salvation (1 Cor. 2:6-8; Rom. 5:1-2; 8:17-25; 29-30; 2 Cor. 4:16-5:10; 1 Thess. 2:12). Every major aspect of his system is related to this concept. When he speaks of the death, resurrection, and exaltation of Christ, he has in mind a Christological pattern (Phil. 2:5-10) which has the most direct bearing on this heavenly destiny of the elect. His discussion of the weakness of the Torah and the resulting chain of sin and death is connected to the question of *how* one can be an "inheritor" of the promises made to Abraham, which he interprets cosmically (Rom. 4:13-15; Gal. 3:15-29). This whole cluster of ideas (Torah, covenants, sin, death, promises, inheritance) provides the basis for his emphasis on justification by faith. This is the *way* one enters the elect community, becomes an inheritor, and is given the hope of glorification. Indeed, Paul's emphasis on grace and gift reaches its most eloquent expression when he focuses on the cosmic destiny of these sons of God and their transformation at the return of Jesus (2 Cor. 4:13-18; Rom. 8:31-39). The giving of the Spirit, "sonship," and "life in the Spirit," all point toward glorification (Rom. 8:15-17; Gal. 4:4-7). The model he presents of suffering, as the "boast" of the true follower of God, points directly to subsequent glorification (Rom. 8:17-18; 5:1-5). His idea of inheriting the kingdom of God and the kind of ethical life this requires is directly related to the change from "flesh and blood" to immortality at the return of Christ (1 Cor. 6:9-11; Gal. 5:15-21; 1 Cor. 15:50). Obviously, one might take any single element of Paul's message and argue that it is *related* to various others, but the ultimate content of the plan of God must be more basic than its "ways and means." Paul's use of the *language* of glorification, in these key contexts, is what is noteworthy. Paul is consumed with *two great insights*--the vision he has had of the exalted and glorified Christ whom he knows to be the crucified man Jesus, whose followers he had once opposed; and his conviction that by grace through faith this same heavenly glorification is the destiny of the elect group--all else falls in between.

Visions and Revelations of the Lord

If Paul's understanding of heavenly glorification is at the core of his message, I now want to ask how his reported experiences of epiphany and ascent might be related to that expectation. The relevant texts are 1 Cor. 9:1; 15:8; Gal. 1:12, 15-16 and 2 Cor.12:1-10.

I first turn to his "conversion" experience.[32] There can be no doubt that Paul's conversion to the sect of Messianists, who were proclaiming that Jesus was raised from the dead and had been exalted to the throne of God, was based on his own experience of having "seen" Jesus, several years after his execution. In 1 Cor. 9:1 he rhetorically asks, "Have I not *seen* (perfect of *horaō*) the Lord?" Here and in 1 Cor. 15:8-10 he is concerned to show that his office as an apostle stems from his vision of the resurrected Jesus and is in line with the witness of the other apostles who came before him. In 1 Cor. 15:8 he writes, "But last of all he *appeared* (aorist passive of *horaō*) to me." Whether Paul thought his own "seeing" the Lord was the same kind of experience as that of the other apostles or not, he clearly means something other than the kind of "appearances" of Jesus in the later tradition (Luke 24:36-43; John 20:26-29) There the emphasis is on the literal "flesh and bones" body that was crucified. These accounts are obviously apologetic and intended to counter the charge that the appearances of Jesus were merely visionary. For Paul it is different. Jesus is no longer flesh and blood, but has become a "life-giving spirit" (1 Cor. 15:45,50). His body is that of a glorious heavenly being (1 Cor. 15:42-50; Phil. 3:20-21), and he sits at the right hand of God in heaven (Rom. 8:34). Since, as we have shown, all the terms that apply to Jesus' present mode of heavenly, glorified existence, apply as well to the elect group awaiting final transformation, then Paul's message in this regard is directly related to what he *saw* at his conversion. Perhaps his experience was something like that reported of Stephen in Acts 7:56--"Behold, I see the heavens opened, and the Son of man [Jesus] standing at the right hand of God!"--but whatever its exact nature, my point is that he identified the glorified one he saw with the crucified man Jesus, and such a vision of glory must have been in his mind when he spoke of the expected glorification of the elect. It was something he had *seen*. In Gal. 1:11-12 he declares:

> I want you to realize, brothers, that the gospel which I preach is not a human gospel, for I did not receive it from man, nor was I taught it, but it came through a *revelation of Jesus Christ.*

Then further in verses 15-16 he says:

> But when the one who set me apart from my mother's womb and called me through his grace, was pleased *to reveal his Son to me* in order that I might preach him among the Gentiles, I did not consult with any human being . . . .

Some scholars would deny that the terms "revelation" and "reveal" here in Galatians refer to visionary experience.[33] The issue seems to be whether or not Paul derived his theology from such visions. These scholars would maintain that Paul disparaged ecstatic experiences and certainly would place no weight on such in his "exposition and defense of the Gospel."[34] It is obvious that Paul refers to his vision of the resurrected Jesus at his conversion. Such an experience might well have involved a verbal revelation as well.[35] Paul elsewhere reports such communications with the Lord (2 Cor. 12:8-9; 1 Thess. 4:15). In this case, the message he received and the vision he saw have everything to do with one another.

In 2 Cor. 12:1 Paul speaks of his *many* "visions and revelations of the Lord," and goes on to recount *one* such experience from fourteen years earlier, his ascent to Paradise, the subject of this book. Certainly his use of the term *apokalupsis* ("revelation") here and in 12:7 refers to visionary experience, which would lend support to my interpretation of Gal. 1:11-16 above. I shall argue below that nothing in the context of 2 Cor. 12 sould lead one to conclude that Paul disparaged such experiences. To be taken up to heaven, to hear and see things "impossible to express," and which "one is not permitted to utter," was a privilege of the highest order. Given Paul's emphasis on the heavenly glorification of the elect to be revealed at the return of Jesus, there is every reason to conclude that this experience, along with that of his initial conversion, would have closely tied in with his gospel message.

Apostolic Authority and Mission

I begin this section with a summary and application of the work of John Schütz on apostolic authority.[36] Schütz carefully distinguishes between the conceptual coordinates power, authority, and legitimacy. Authority is an *interpretation* of power while legitimacy is an interpretation of authority. Power then, has priority (like Weber's *charisma*), and is the source of authority, while authority interprets power and makes it accessible. Legitimacy is a formalization of authority, an attempt to communicate authority and make it accessible. Paul comes before such a formalization; thus to understand Paul as an apostle, we are not concerned with the concept of legitimacy, but with authority itself, i.e., Paul's *own* sense of apostolic authority as seen in his letters. We have no normative concept of "apostle" from Paul's own time with which he can be compared, so how does Paul interpret his power and upon what grounds does he view it as an ultimate source of authority? Paul's letters are a combination of proclamation and parenesis (exhortation). As he seeks to mold and control the beliefs and conduct of his churches, the range of subjects he covers in our limited collection of letters is wide. A partial breakdown would include:

1. sexual conduct in general (1 Thess. 4:3-8; 1 Cor. 7:1-7; Gal. 5:19; 1 Cor. 5:9 -10; 6:9
2. frequency of sexual intercourse (1 Cor. 7:1-7)
3. incest (1 Cor. 5:1-5)
4. homosexuality (1 Cor. 6:9)
5. prostitution (1 Cor. 6:15-18)
6. celibacy (1 Cor. 7:8-9)
7. marital states (1 Cor. 7)

8. separation and divorce (1 Cor. 7:12-15)
9. alms and support of the ministry (1 Cor. 9:1-14; 16:1-4; Rom. 15:15-29; 2 Cor. 8-9; Gal. 6:6; Rom. 12:13; 16:1-2)
10. non-retaliation (1 Thess. 5:15; Rom. 12:14-21)
11. community expulsions and lawsuits (1 Cor. 5; 6:1-8)
12. vegetarianism, idol meat, alcohol (1 Cor. 8:1-13; 10:23-31; Rom. 14
13. slavery (1 Cor. 7:20-24)
14. circumcision (1 Cor. 7:18-19)
15. relations with outside society (1 Cor. 5:9; 10:27-31)
16. dress/hair length (1 Cor. 11:1-16)
17. regulations for meetings (1 Cor. 11:17-34; 14)
18. observance of holy days (Rom. 14:5-6; Gal. 4:10)
19. relations with civil government (Rom. 13:1-7)
20. paying taxes (Rom. 13:7)
21. jobs and employment (1 Thess. 4:11-12)

When he sets forth and defends his positions on matters of belief or practice, he is concerned to draw implications from his gospel message (making use of dialectical argument, appeal to tradition, and exegesis of scripture); but often as not he simply appeals to his authority, *demanding* imitation, submission and obedience. I will argue that Paul exerts this kind of personal authority based upon his understanding of his special role as an apostle.

Imitate Me

In response to the fragmented and confused state of affairs in the Corinthian congregation Paul writes:

> I am not writing you to shame you, but to admonish you as beloved children. For if you have numerous guides in Christ, you do not have many fathers, since *I begot you* in Christ Jesus through the gospel. I urge you, *imitate me*! This is why I sent Timothy to you . . . to *remind you of my ways* in Christ as I teach them in all the churches. Some are arrogant as though I were not coming to you, but I will arrive soon, if the Lord wills, and I will ascertain the *power* of these puffed up ones, *not their talk*. For the Kingdom of God does not exist on talk but on power! What do you prefer? Shall I come to you with a rod, or with love in a spirit of gentleness? (1 Cor. 4:14-21)

These verses are paradigmatic of the way Paul exercises authority in the churches he has founded. His position is that of the *auctor*.[37] Although he recognizes the legitimate role others may play in carrying forward his work as "father," or in building upon the foundation of the master builder, his authority remains preeminent (see 1 Cor. 3:10; Rom. 15:18-21). At times this position is reflected in language which is intimate, tender, and deeply personal. He reminds the Thessalonians:

> But we were gentle[38] among you, like a nurse caring for her children, so having such yearning love for you, we were ready to share not only the gospel of God with you, but our very selves, since you had become so dear to us (1 Thess. 2:7-8).

Further on, he uses the image of a father with his children (2:11). Even in a situation as heated as that in Galatia, he tenderly appeals to them as "my little children," picturing himself as a mother in labor pains over them (3:19). He pleads desperately with the Corinthians:

> Our mouth is open to you Corinthians, our heart is wide . . . open your hearts to us; we have wronged no one, we have corrupted no one, we have not taken advantage of anyone. I do not say this to condemn you, for I said before that you are in our hearts . . . (2 Cor. 6:11; 7:2-3a).

Twice he reminds them that his authority is for building up, not for punishing (2 Cor. 10:8; 13:10). Often he mentions the return of Jesus and the overflowing joy he will have in presenting them to Christ, faithful and blameless (1 Thess. 2:17-20; 3:8-13; 2 Cor. 1:14; Phil. 1:10; 2:16). At other times his tone is severe, threatening, and overbearing. This is particularly clear in 2 Cor. 10-13, where he seems uncertain of his ability to maintain his position:

> I beg you that when I am present I may not have to be overbearing with the kind of persuasion I plan on employing against those who accuse us of living on a human plane (10:2).

> For even if I boast a bit of our authority (which the Lord gave for building up, not for destroying you) I will not be put to shame . . . . let such people realize that what we *say* by letter when away, we *do* when present! (10:8, 11)

> I warned those who sinned before and all the others, and I warn them now while absent, as I did then when I was there--on my second visit, that if I come again *I will not spare them*--since you want proof that Christ is speaking through me (12:2-3a).

Intrinsic to the authority of the *auctor* are the concepts of imitation and obedience. As father and founder, Paul exhorts the Corinthians to "imitate me" and sent Timothy as his representative to remind them "of my ways" as taught in all the churches. The apostle is the mediator of divine power in the world and the guarantor of the "success of the enterprise."[39] He not only speaks "in" or "for" Christ, but in a representative sense *is* Christ manifest in the world. To disregard him is to disregard God who has given him this position. Faithfulness to God is indeed faithfulness to God's message, with all its implications. But in a practical sense this faithfulness is demonstrated (or judged) by submission to the apostle. The source of authority is not merely "rational" but "irrational" or ultimate.[40]   This is nowhere more forcefully illustrated than in the language Paul uses in 1 Cor. 5:3-5 in dealing with the reported case of incest within the congregation. He writes:

> For although I am absent in body, *I am present in spirit*, and as present, *I have already pronounced judgment* in the name of the Lord Jesus upon the man who has committed such a deed. When you are assembled, and *my spirit is present* with the power of our Lord Jesus, deliver this man to Satan for the destruction of the flesh, that his spirit may be saved on the day of the Lord.[41]

The apostolic *ego* is the key point to be noted here. *Paul* passes the judgment "in the name of the Lord" and *Paul's* spirit is present "with the power of the Lord." The prepositional phrases are clearly subordinate to the immediate manifestation of divine power in the community. Such language is extraordinary and implies an interpretation of power quite different from later church concepts of apostolic succession and legitimacy.[42]

1 Cor. 11:1-16 is of particular interest in this regard, even though much of Paul's argument will likely remain obscure to us.[43] Paul begins the chapter with his formulaic command, "Be imitators of me, as I am of Christ." In the following verse he commends the community for remembering him in every matter and maintaining the traditions (*paradoseis*) which he had delivered to them.[44] He then proceeds to detail instructions regarding how women are to wear their hair. He concludes by asserting:

> If anyone would like to argue, we recognize no other practice, nor do the churches of God! (11:16).

He concludes the longest section of this letter (chapters 12-14) with a similar, though more *forceful*, declaration. After giving detailed instructions regarding the proper use of "spiritual gifts" in the assembly and pointedly ordering that women are to remain silent, he declares:

> If anyone considers himself to be a prophet or a spiritual one, let him acknowledge that what I write you is a *command of the Lord*. If anyone disregards this then he is disregarded! (14:37-38).[45]

What should be noted here is that the *final test* of spirituality, in a situation in which *various* charismatics set forth their claims, is submission to the authority of the apostle. Paul speaks unequivocally for the Lord--his voice is to be heeded and his life imitated as the locus of divine power for his communities.

The tension he feels in resolving issues of controversy in his churches is particularly clear in 1 Cor. 7, where he offers both advice and directive regarding marital states, divorce and states of life in general. Several of these issues, raised explicitly or implicitly by the Corinthians (7:1), demanded a specificity that went beyond what might have been deduced or argued from the theological content of his gospel proclamation. Although he does label what he writes regarding whether it is better to be married or single as his opinion, he pushes his own position forcefully and fortifies this "opinion" with the tactful phrase, "And I think that I have the Spirit of God" (vv. 6, 25, 40). The juxtaposition of verses 10-11 and verses 12-16 is most interesting:

> To the unmarried *I give order*, not I, but the Lord, that the wife should not separate from her husband (but if she does she is to remain single or else be reconciled to her husband), and the husband is not to divorce his wife (10-11).

Here Paul relates *his command* to a saying of Jesus which he has received from the tradition.[46] He then introduces his further discussion with the parallel phrase:

> To the rest, *I say*, not the Lord . . . (12a).

The clear force of this is not merely that he has nothing in the tradition regarding this matter, but that he equates what he sets forth in the following verses (12-16) *with* a saying of Jesus. In fact, verse 15 offers a reason for divorce which moves beyond the logion of Jesus, and taken at face value, contradicts it. Paul then, is willing to legislate, in matters as weighty as divorce, and is willing to go beyond a traditional saying of Jesus. To write "I say" or "the Lord says," for Paul, equivalently represents the authority of God. This is not to say that he exercises such authority indiscriminately, but that in various ways and in various contexts his claim to such is clear. In verses 17-24 he takes up the questions of circumcision and slavery. He declares:

> Let each person lead the life which the Lord has assigned him, each as God has called him. This is *my rule* in all the churches (7:17).

In each case he does offer theological grounds to support what he orders (vv. 19, 22-23), but his use of the verb *diatassomai* ("This is my rule") is forceful and characteristic.[47] He uses it twice more in a similar way in this letter. First in 11:34, following a series of responses to questions and situations in the community. He concludes:

> Regarding the other matters, I will *give orders* when I come.

Then in 16:1 he directs them to prepare the collection of funds he was to take to Jerusalem. This verse, with its matter-of-fact tone of authority should be compared with the complex appeal he makes regarding the same collection in 2 Cor. 8-9. There he obviously feels under fire and fears he has lost hold on portions of the group. He exercises the utmost tact, appealing to a "rational" source of authority.[48]

It is in the portions of this collection of correspondence (now preserved in 2 Corinthians) where Paul's authority has been directly threatened by rival "apostles" and he is pushed to the wall, that the direct demand for "obedience" is especially evident. In his reconciling letter to the Corinthians (1:1-2:13; 7:5-16) he refers to his previous "letter of tears":

> Because of this I wrote in order to test you in everything, *to see if you are obedient in everything* (2:9).

He echoes the same concern in 7:15 in commenting on the reception of Titus as his envoy:

> And his [Titus'] heart goes out all the more to you as he recalls the *obedience of you all*, as you received him with *fear and trembling.*

He had introduced this theme of "obedience" in the previous letter (10:1-6):

> We overthrow argument [i.e., with the weapons of divine power-- v. 4] and every proud obstacle to the knowledge of God,. and take every thought captive to obey Christ, having prepared to punish every disobedience, *when your obedience is complete* (10:5 -6)

The destructive use of his authority which he threatens in 10:8 and again in 13:10, is intended for the outsider or the opponent, not for the obedient child who imitates the father. The situation reflected in 2 Cor. 10-13 is so desperate that the "children" themselves are in danger of moving into this category, and thus suffering the destruction of divine power mediated by the apostle. This is very serious business (remember the language of 1 Cor. 5:5). Obedience to Christ is to be gauged by obedience to the apostle, as we have seen earlier. The ideal is well expressed in the Philippian letter, where Paul feels strong support and acceptance of his authority:

> Thus my beloved ones, as you have *always obeyed*, so do so now, not only when I am present, but even more when I am absent-- accomplish your salvation *with fear and trembling!* (2:12).

Such obedience "with fear and trembling" is ultimately directed toward God, but immediately manifested in the degree of submission to the apostle. It is the test and indicator of faithfulness and thus the guarantee of participation in full salvation. Such imitative submission is a test for Paul as well, that his labor was not in vain (Phil. 2:16). I have already cited the passages where he speaks of the joy they will have together at the return of Jesus from heaven. His hope is that he can present a blameless and obedient community to

26

Christ, as fruit of his labor. But it is quite obvious that no individual who rebels against Paul and rejects his authority, will be included in that gathering.

The tone and approach adopted by Paul in asserting "his ways" in his congregations varies in any given situation according to the *degree of acceptance he thinks he has from the group.* This accounts for the broadly different ways his authority comes across in various letters. 1 Thessalonians reflects a high degree of acceptance. Although there may have been some criticism of the character and motives of the absent apostle (thus the mild defense in 2:1-12), it likely stemmed from *outside* persecutors. Paul is mainly concerned with encouraging and building up the fledgling group in the face of such opposition. The general tone of the letter is warm and deeply personal. In the parenetical section (chaps. 4 and 5) he exhorts and encourages them (4:1), gives them "instruction" (4:2, 11), warns them (4:6), corrects their misunderstanding concerning the resurrection of the dead (4:13-5:12) and closes with a series of imperatives (5:12-22). Several times he mentions that they are already following the right course and asks them to do so "more and more" (4:1; 9-10; 5:11). His most insistent language comes in 5:27--"I adjure you by the Lord that this letter be read to all the brethren!" All of the elements of Paul's apostolic authority are evident, but the tone and approach is mild. They are to "imitate" their "father" (2:11; 4:1); what they are told is the "word of God," not of men (2:13; 4:8, 15). But the enemies are *outside*, and the harsh language, of which Paul is so capable, is directly against them, i.e., in this case the Jews (2:14-16).

Philippians reflects a quite similar manner of asserting authority. The tone is gentle, encouraging and deeply personal. They *are*, nonetheless, *to obey and imitate* the apostle:

> What you have learned and received and heard and seen *in me-- do!* And the God of peace will be with you (4:9).

> Brothers, join in *imitating me,* and mark those who so live as you have an example in us (3:17).

These imperatives offer excellent examples of how Paul views the model follower of Christ, the one assured of God's favor. I have noted previously his exhortation to obedience in 2:12. The polemical section of the letter (3:2-11, 17-19), although similar in language to sections of Galatians and 2 Corinthians, and quite harsh in tone, is again clearly directed against outsiders. Paul is confident that the group is receptive to him.

1 Corinthians represents a midway situation. There are internal factions within the congregation, and the language he uses is considerably heated. There is some doubt in Paul's mind about the degree of submission he will receive. This accounts for the much stronger language, some of which I have already quoted above. The same elements are present (Paul as father, the

idea of imitation, commands and directives), but they come across in a more demanding and absolute way than in 1 Thessalonians or Philippians. Overall, though, Paul still perceives himself to be in charge.

It is in sections of 2 Corinthians and in Galatians where one finds a changed approach--though the opponents Paul faces are different. Here the ground has shifted. In Galatians he uses hyperbolic language with a full repertoire of cursing, sarcasm, dire threats and warnings:[49]

> I am amazed that you are so quickly deserting him who called you . . . (1:6a).

> If anyone is preaching to you a gospel contrary to the one you received, let him be damned! (1:9b)[50]

> O foolish Galatians! Who has bewitched you! (3:1)

> I have confidence in the Lord that you will take *no other view than mine* and that the one troubling you will bear his condemnation, whoever he is! (5:10)

> I wish the ones unsettling you would mutilate themselves! [i.e., their penises by a slip of the circumcision knife] (5:12)

In this situation the issue is sharply defined--must a Gentile convert to Judaism and observe the Torah in order to be saved? It is not, then, a simple case of Paul asserting his position as father to the community. Although the opponents are outsiders, they have clearly made internal gains. He puts forth arguments to support his case (especially in chaps. 3 and 4). But still, there is a very strong *personal* appeal, particularly in 3:12-20; 5:10 and 6:17. He knows it is possible that he may have lost his power in the group. Therefore, he must defend both the content of his message "rationally," *and* the unquestionable authority given to him as an apostle of God.

However, it is the situation reflected behind the texts we now have collected in 2 Corinthians that best illustrates Paul's understanding of his authority per se. Despite the impossibility of reconstructing the identity and theology of his opponents with any certainty, the situation is desperate and his hold is weakened over portions of the group. The key chapters are 10-13. Paul's efforts to *re*-assert his position as "father" to the congregation exhibit a different tone and approach than that of any of his other letters. It is here that he sets forth his most complex and personal defense of his authority as an apostle, making an outright *demand* for their obedience and submission to him. It is important therefore, that his ascent account, which comes in this section of the letter, be understood in its proper context.

In all of his letters, despite the differing tones and variety of approaches and situations, the essential interpretation of power is the same--to please

God and be accepted by Christ at his return one must live presently in imitation of and submission to the apostle whom he has sent. Paul himself represents the working of the true Spirit in the community.

An obvious related question is the extent to which Paul's mediation of divine power is shared by every other person "in Christ," to use his language. All possess the same Spirit (1 Cor. 12:12-13). The manifestations of this Spirit are spread throughout the whole body (1 Cor. 12, 14). The community as a whole is "called by God" and is participating in the mission and work of God in the world. There is certainly an extent to which the "children" are *like* the "father." That is the obvious force of the notion of imitation. The task of the father involves an "augmentation" of the power he represents.[51] Yet *all* are not apostles (1 Cor. 12:29). *All* are not fathers (1 Cor. 4:15). No one else could have used the language toward the community which I have just examined. The issue is who is to be ultimately heard and heeded, imitated and obeyed, in a situation of *shared charismata.* Rational appeal and argument can work in certain situations, and Paul makes full use of these, but when rivals also claim to have the "Spirit" and speak for Christ the lines of battle can become very blurred. This is the case in 2 Cor. 10-13.

Sign of a True Apostle

One could hardly point to a more difficult portion of the Pauline corpus than 2 Cor. 10-13. There is the problem of style; Paul's language and lines of argument are extremely complex and difficult.[52] The identity of his opponents seems beyond our abilities to reconstruct.[53] Does Paul face a new situation from that of 1 Corinthians? What might be the origin of these opponents--the Jerusalem church, the diasporic Christian mission, or the Corinthian community itself? Are they best characterized as Judaizers, Pneumatics, Gnostics (or gnostics) or some combination of these? How does Paul differ from his opposition? In what ways is he similar? John Gunther, in an extraordinary job of cataloging, offers thirteen categories of identification of these opponents, reflecting the positions of thirty-nine scholars![54] He lists: Wandering Jewish preachers taking over the Gnostic opposition of 1 Cor.; Jewish Gnostic Christians of the same sort as in 1 Cor.; Pneumatic-libertine Gnostics; Gnostics; Alexandrian syncretistic antinomian pneumatics; Jewish-pagan-Christian gnostics; Hellenistic Jewish Christians; Non-Judaizing Jewish Christians; Palestinian Jewish-Christian Gnostics; Jewish Christian syncretists with Gnostic elements; Jerusalem Judaizers; Palestinian Jews--not Judaizers in the Galatian sense; Judaizers; Judaizers and pneumatic Gnostics. It is obvious that such a list is inflated, overlapping, and imprecise, however, its very unwieldiness illustrates the difficulties of such attempts at identification. How one evaluates the ascent account is generally related to one's characterization of the position of the opponents. Without attempting to cover all the nuances of such identification, I want to isolate several of the main lines of interpretation as they are related to this question of how Paul regarded his ascent experience.

29

First, there is the view that the opponents were criticizing Paul as an ecstatic visionary who relied on his "revelations" to legitimatize his apostleship, but lacked the authorization of the Jerusalem church with its connection with the historical Jesus. Most often they would be seen as "Judaizers" (Baur, Schoeps), perhaps similar to those in Galatia, and either commissioned by the Jerusalem apostles (Baur) or at least claiming authority from them.[55] This interpretation generally brings together Paul's defense of his call (Gal. 1:11-12); his remarks about the "reputed pillars" of the church (Gal. 2:6-9); his insistence that he is not inferior to the original apostles; his claim that he too has "seen the Lord" (1 Cor. 9:1); and his reference to no longer "knowing Jesus according to the flesh" (2 Cor. 5:16). Thus, the "superlative apostles" contrasted themselves with him as though he had no rank (2 Cor. 11:5; 12:11). Schoeps has argued that the pseudo-Clementine texts, while reflecting a much later stage of anti-Paulinism, preserve for us, in compact form, the essential arguments of these Judaizers at Corinth (whom, according to Schoeps, Paul faced at Galatia as well). He relies on the debate between Peter and Paul (who appears under the name of the heretic Simon) in *Homily* 17. Peter argues that "Paul's" claim to "revelations" of the Lord have no validity:

> The personal knowledge and the personal instruction of the true prophet gives certainty; vision leaves us in uncertainty. For the latter may spring from a misleading spirit which feigns to be what it is not.[56]

I see two major weaknesses with this position. First, there is no convincing evidence in these chapters, nor in 1 and 2 Corinthians as a whole (despite the reference to a "different gospel" in 11:4; cf. Gal. 1:6-9), of a Judaizing position akin to that of the opponents at Galatian who demanded that Gentiles be circumcised and keep the Torah. The way Paul goes about defending his apostleship simply does not correspond to that kind of opposition.[57] Second, even though Schoeps' appeal to the pseudo-Clementine materials has a certain attraction, it seems unlikely that Paul would *appeal* to his "visions and revelations" (even if "speaking as a fool"--11:21) if such visionary experience was the very point at issue. The rhetorical subtleties which he employs in his "Narrenrede" (irony, sarcasm, parody) indicate something much more complex is at stake.[58] Paul is pressed to *boast* of his revelations precisely because his opponents were making claims on the basis of their own ecstatic experiences.

Schmithals holds the position that the opponents were genuine Gnostics of Palestinian origin who boasted of pneumatic-ecstatic experiences of all kinds. He argues for a "one front battle" with Paul facing the same Gnostic opposition throughout the Corinthian correspondence. Such opponents would have charged that Paul was not a Pneumatic (at least on their level) and therefore not an apostle. Paul defends himself against such a charge both in 1 Cor. 14 and 2 Cor. 12. In both cases he does not reject such experiences; indeed, he must show that he has them "more than you all" (1 Cor. 14:18) and in "abundance" (2 Cor. 12:1, 7). Schmithals, however, holds that he *depreciates* them as expressions of individual or "personal religion," fundamentally different in character from his Damascus revelation, and of no value to the community as a whole.[59] Thus, in 2 Cor. 12:1-10, he is *unwillingly* pressed to meet his opponents on their own ground, "foolishly" boasting of an abundance of visions and revelations.

Dieter Georgi, arguing from 2 Cor. 2:14-7:4 and 10-13, has proposed that Paul faces a new group of opponents who had come into the community after he wrote 1 Corinthians. He characterizes them as wandering Hellenistic Jewish pneumatics who viewed Moses and Jesus on the model of a *theios anēr*, glorying in their revelations and miracles as demonstrations of their "power" (*dunamis*). They are part of an organized Christian missionary movement, stemming from diasporic Jewish-Christian circles.[60] Paul, while ironically boasting of his own pneumatic experience, stands in sharpest contrast to them with his emphasis on the crucified Jesus and his model of the suffering apostle who has power in weakness (2 Cor. 4:8-12; 6:4-10; 11:23-29; 12:10).[61]

While Schmithals opposes Georgi's overall thesis, he agrees that the false apostles in Corinth are the type of traveling Pneumatics which Georgi describes.[62] However, he would insist that they are *Gnostic* apostles and that Paul faces their opposition *throughout* the Corinthian correspondence, not merely in 2 Corinthians.

There does seem to be a growing consensus among scholars on a number of key points. First, the lines of battle are drawn over the issue of *who* is a true apostle--what Käsemann calls the question of "*legitimität.*" Paul's authority has been questioned and he is pressed to defend himself (though strictly speaking he denies this--2 Cor. 12:19) in contrast to his opponents, whom he asserts are false apostles (11:13) and servants Satan (11:15). Second, contrary to Schmithals, a new situation has developed from that reflected in 1 Corinthians.[63] Third, this new group of "apostles" are certainly of Jewish background (3:7-18; 11:21-23), taking pride in such identity, though probably unlike the Judaizers at Galatia.[64] Whether they are Hellenistic Jewish Christians from the diaspora or Palestinian Christians from the Jerusalem church seems impossible to resolve. Finally, and this point is crucial, *both* Paul *and* his opponents claimed pneumatic powers, the ability to work miracles and various experiences of vision and revelation (Georgi, Schmithals, Käsemann, Bornkamm, Oostendorp, Friedrich, and Barrett all agree here).

At issue then is *how* Paul, in 2 Cor. 10-13, goes about defending his apostleship against these newly arrived Jewish opponents who are also claiming pneumatic powers; and specifically, for this study, what is the point of his mentioning his ascent to Paradise in such a context? E. Earle Ellis offers a succinct characterization of this type of situation:

The Pauline mission was an enterprise of pneumatics, persons

31

who claimed special understanding of scripture and who experienced manifestations of inspired, ecstatic speech and of visions and revelations. The primary opposition to that mission arose from within a segment of the ritually strict *Hebraioi* in the Jerusalem church and with variations in nuance continued to pose, sometimes as a counter mission and sometimes as an infiltrating influence, a settled and persistent "other" gospel. Each group claimed to be the true voice of Jesus, each claimed to give the true *gnōsis* of God, and on occasion, each made its higher appeal to apostolic status. It was, in a word, a *battle of prophets*, and the congregation was called upon to choose--Paul or his opposition.[65]

Most scholars have concluded that Paul, in facing such opposition, to one degree or another, *disparaged* pneumatic experiences, refusing to allow such to serve as a basis for validating his authority. The following comment by C. K. Barrett on Paul's ascent experience typifies this viewpoint:

> It is true that xii.2ff describes an experience in which Paul was caught up to heaven and heard words which he was not allowed to communicate to his fellow men; . . . It remains significant that, to find a suitably impressive example of visions and revelations of the Lord (xii.1), he goes back fourteen years (xii.2); such raptures did not happen to him every other week . . . . . To Paul, the spiritual world was unmistakably real, and from time to time he experienced it in an ecstatic way; but so far from cultivating this kind of experience *he rather disparaged it*, and laid no weight on it in his exposition and defense of the Gospel.[66]

He argues that the apostle's legitimacy appears not in the power of his personality, not in such ecstatic experiences or revelations, not in his commissioning by the right ecclesiastical authorities, but only in the extent to which his life and preaching represent the crucified Jesus. Accordingly, even if Paul must reluctantly compare himself with his opponents, ultimately he refuses to do so, "boasting " only in his weaknesses and sufferings. Bornkamm essentially follows this same line of interpretation.[67] I have already noted how Schmithals argues that Paul depreciates such experiences as expressions of individual religion. W. D. Davies holds that the ascent experience is not of "primary importance" and that Paul never makes any vision he may have had (as the "Hellenistic pneumatics" must have done) the basis for any of his teaching.[68] James Dunn, while admitting the obvious, that Paul "was no stranger to ecstatic experiences," says the question of real moment is whether they were important to Paul. He concludes:

> Certainly Paul knows experiences which take him out of himself--even, it perhaps seemed at the time, out of the body (II Cor. 12:2ff.). But such experiences are the *least significant* for

Paul; it is the daily experience of weakness that finds him closest to God and the power of God most effective through him (II Cor. 12:9f.; 13:4).[69]

He goes on to say, "Paul derived his authority as an apostle not from the inspiration of the present but from the decisive events of the past which remained determinative for believers."[70] He is referring to authoritative tradition of Jesus, his once-for-all revelation or appearance to Paul whereby he was commissioned to take the message to the Gentiles, and establish the church through that ministry. Russell Spittler, in an article appropriately called, "The Limits of Ecstasy," concludes:

> The paradise rapture would not even have been mentioned now but for the fact that Paul was forced to do so . . . that is, he was forced to respond to attacks on his apostolic authority based on charges (whether expressed, or implied in the extravagant ecstatic claims of the opponents) of his ecstatic or pneumatic deficiency. The thrust of his polemic is by no means an attempt to outdo the opponents by detailing a superior ecstatic experience. Rather, and still "speaking as a fool," he inverts the very criterion of his opponents by saying in essence that ecstasy is no proper cause for *kauchesis* nor does it provide any adequate apostolic accreditation.[71]

A. T. Lincoln, in a very comprehensive treatment of the passage, acknowledges that such an experience must have been "outstanding" and "highly valued" by Paul, yet goes on to conclude:

> In this context it becomes clear that Paul introduces his visionary experience of heaven only in order to show that it is not such experiences on which he relies for evidence of his apostleship.[72]

I could cite any number of other scholars who draw similar conclusions, including the most recent study by William Baird.[73]

My own position runs directly counter to this trend of modern interpretation. The resolution of the question must involve at least three lines of inquiry. First, there is the question of the exegesis of the text itself. Does Paul's overall defense in 2 Cor. 10-13, and the way in which he brings in the ascent experience, indicate that he disparaged such revelations, or that he is, in fact, defending his authority as an apostle on the basis of such? Second, in a wider context, with regard to Paul's overall understanding of revelation and authority, what would be the significance of this particular experience? And finally, is it important that Paul mentions an *ascent to heaven* when he comes to "visions and revelations," and not just any pneumatic experience, not even his initial vision and call at his conversion (as in Galatians)? This third question relates to an ever broader inquiry--the

33

significance of ascent as a religious experience in the Hellenistic period. I will take this up in the following chapter. At this point I will argue that for Paul the experience of ascent to Paradise was important and did serve to confirm his self-understanding of his authority as an apostle, and further, that it is significant that he tells of a journey to heaven, and not just any ecstatic experience.

Throughout these chapters Paul exhibits fierce indignation and asserts his authority to the uttermost. His invective amounts to a "declaration of war" against those who *fail to submit*.[74] He warns the community (i.e., anyone who would interpret his "weakness" as a lack of divine power) in 10:11, "Let these people understand that what we *say* by letter when absent, we *do* when present!" His purpose in *writing* is not ultimately to defend himself before them (13:19), but to give them opportunity to correct their ways and submit to him *before* he makes his visit (12:21; 13:10), so that he will not *have to be* severe in his use of the authority given to him by Christ (12:10). There is a *sense* in which Paul is in complete control of the situation. He knows that he might have lost a portion of the group, as I have discussed earlier, thus his tone is severe and desperate. But in any final analysis, Paul can not lose. He has no doubt of his authority from the Lord, including the power "to destroy" if necessary (10:8; 13:10). His discussion *begins and ends* on this note. He wants those who have been influenced by the opponents to "mend their ways" and "complete their obedience" (13:11; 10:6) *before* he arrives. For the opponents and those who will not come around, there is no hope. They are "false apostles," "deceitful workers," and servants of Satan himself. He confidently declares that they will suffer an end corresponding to their deeds (11:13-15).[75] Precisely what form this threatened punishment of the disobedient is to take we cannot say. I think it unlikely that he has in mind judgment at the coming of Christ. Reacting to the charge of his enemies, he dispels any notions of "meekness" by speaking of the boldness that *he* intends to show against his enemies when *he* comes (10:2). The military language of 10:3-6 is more than rhetorical display. Paul plans to take some kind of *action* when he arrives. He speaks of "weapons" which have "divine power to destroy," using terms which he often associates with his *own* apostolic office (10:8; 12:9; 13:1-4, 10). The kind of scene described in 1 Cor. 5:3-5, where the man is to be "'delivered to Satan" for destruction is probably our best indication of what he contemplates. As Morton Smith has shown, our best parallels for understanding this kind of talk and action are in the magical papyri.[76] In 4:18-21 he had spoken of the arrogance of some who did not seem bothered by his threats to "come" to them; he offered them the choice of gentleness or a rod, and reminded them of the divine "power" at his disposal. In 2 Cor. 10-13 the situation is more desperate and Paul is ready to act. Even though Paul does take up a certain kind of ironic defense of himself in 11:1-12:10, the overall tone of the chapters is one of full confidence to deal with those who have attached themselves to the opponents. With all of this boldness he still makes the most tender appeal. He reminds them how he loves them and how he is willing to "be spent" for them (12:15). He only wants to build them up, and is disappointed that they have not returned his love and "commended" him themselves (12:11).

One charge made against Paul was that he was bold and forceful in his letters, but that when actually present was weak and unimpressive (10:2, 10; 11:16). It was said that he had "overextended" himself in various ways as he sought to exercise his apostolic authority (10:14). This might be related to his policy of not taking financial support from them, which some saw as proof that he did not have the full rights of an apostle (11:7-11; 12:13-18). There is every indication that some in the group went on to question whether Paul had the right to be called an apostle at all, asserting that he did not meet "the test" in comparison to others (10:18; 13:3). This probably involved an appeal by the opponents to "signs, wonders, and mighty works" (12:12), as well as to "visions and revelations" (12:1), which they felt demonstrated their own power and standing as apostles. They, at the same time, took pride in their Jewish background as Hebrews, Israelites, and descendants of Abraham (11:22).[77]

Several of these charges Paul refutes directly, using a technique of denial and reversal. It is *they* who have overextended themselves, not he; he was the "first to reach them" and is their founder, while these false apostles "boast" of work done in another man's field of labor (10:13-16). He did not take money from them because he loved love, like a parent who sacrifices for his children. He showed no trace of craftiness or guile (11:7-12; 12:13-18). The opponents, on the other hand, take all kinds of advantage over them, seeking to enslave them, and would never adopt Paul's way of not "burdening" the church, because they are greedy for the gain it brings them (11:12-21).

The crux of his response, however, involves the subtle and shifting use of four key terms: weakness (*astheneia*); power (*dunamis*); boasting (*kauchēsis*) and foolishness (*aphrosunē*).[78] Paul's concern is to make it clear that he is not the least bit *"inferior"* to the opponents, whom he sarcastically labels as "super-apostles." The core of his defense begins and ends with this assertion (11:5; 12:11). His argument is very difficult because of a complex mix of sarcasm, irony and parody. He reverses the level of the discussion, so that at various points he is operating on two different planes, with the key terms of the discussion carrying different meanings. At one and the same time he meets the opponents on their own ground, and *denies the validity of* that very ground, by setting forth his authority on a different level.

He charges that the opponents operate *kata sarka*, "on a worldly plane" (10:18). They attempt to do battle with him on that level (10:2), claiming that Paul fails to meet the "test" (*dokimos*). This idea of a test or proof is important in these chapters (10:18; 13:3, 5-7). The Corinthians wanted "proof" that Christ was speaking in Paul. But he closes his letter by asking *them* to examine themselves, to see if it might be they who have failed the "test." This test is finally whether or not they submit to him. Their operation on this worldly plane causes them to boast over "worldly things" (11:18). They compare and measure themselves with one another (10:12), *commending themselves* on the basis of their pneumatic powers and their Jewish connections (10:18). They see themselves as having power, while Paul is judged as weak and unimpressive (10:10; 11:6).

Speaking as a "fool" (11:1, 16-17, 21; 12:11), Paul is able to engage the opponents point by point on *this* level. He too can boast of worldly things. He is a Hebrew, an Israelite, a descendent of Abraham, a servant of Christ (11:22-23). He too can speak of "visions and revelations" which he has experienced (12:1). But in doing so he actually cuts the ground from under them. First, he denies that they *are*, in fact, servants of Christ in the first place. They are evil and deceitful ministers, *false* apostles, who are serving Satan, *not* Christ (11:13-15). And as for their revelations, he implies in 12:6 that such claims were based on falsehood. By this he does not mean that their visions are fraudulent, but as servants of Satan, their claim that their power is from Christ is necessarily a lie. Paul insists that "another spirit" stands behind their manifestation of pneumatic power (11:4)! His point is that since his *many* "visions and revelations" are *truly* "of the Lord," even if he did wish to meet them on this point, he would at least be speaking the truth. But ultimately he refuses to operate on such a level, this level of comparison and boasting of *himself* and what he has experienced (12:5) instead he shifts the ground. He says in 10:18, "for it is not the man who *approves himself* that is accepted (*dokimos*), but the one whom the *Lord approves.*" They had charged that he was weak (10:10). Paul and turns the charge against them. If he "must boast" (11:30; 12:1) then he will boast of this--*his weaknesses* (11:30; 12:5). On the "worldly plane" this would be an admission of defeat, but in terms of "whom the Lord approves," weakness turns out to mean divine power, the power of Christ himself (12:9-10). It is in this context that he mentions his ascent to Paradise--coming between 11:30 and 12:10.[79] Paradoxically, this extraordinary and exalted revelation brought "weakness":

> And to keep me from being too elated because the revelations were so marvelous (*huperbolē*), a thorn in the flesh was given to me, a *messenger of Satan* (*aggelos*), to harass me, to keep me from being too elated (12:7).

I have taken *huperbolē* to refer to the greatness or privileged nature of the revelations (i.e., things both impossible and unlawful to utter--v. 4).[80] On Paul's celebrated "thorn in the flesh," the speculations are endless and at times sound like entries in a medical encyclopedia.[81] This focus on the phrase "thorn in the flesh" throws one off. There is no indication here that Paul is writing about some physical ailment he suffered. Perhaps our best clue is what he plainly says, an *angel of Satan* (i.e., a demon) was allowed to afflict him (without specifying what such harassment involved). Paul knows that he too could fall victim to the temptation of self-exultation, especially because of such a privileged experience. At first he asks the Lord to send this Satanic one away, not once, but *three different times* (12:8, like Jesus facing his own temptation in Gethsemane-- Mark 14:32-42). Each time he is told the same paradoxical message by Jesus himself:

> My grace is sufficient for you, my *power* is brought to fullness
> in weakness (12:9).

Paul is able to mention the experience, obliquely, using the third person, because *he is nothing* (12:11).[82] It was nothing *he* could boast of, but rather something *granted to him by the Lord* (12:1, 5).[83] On a "worldly plane" such a privileged experience means "weakness," but in terms of "whom the Lord approves" it brings a fullness of divine power. Paul, of course, relates this paradox of weakness/power to Jesus' death on the cross: "For he was crucified in weakness, but lives by the power of God" (13:4). Paul is like Christ. Though he is "weak," he will "live with him by the power of God,"when it comes to dealing with them (13:4). The opponents had charged that he was weak and that he boasted too much of his authority (10:8-10). His answer is based on his experience. Yes, he *is* weak, but that weakness signifies that the power of Christ is fully displayed through him; yes he *does* boast, but not of himself, he boasts "in the Lord" (10:17; 12:1, 5).

By recounting this revelation Paul is not trying to assert the validity of suffering as a criterion of apostleship, contrasting it with visionary ecstatic experience. That is not the way his argument runs. Rather he is setting forth two *ways of commendation*. There are those who commend themselves, boasting on their own behalf, and there are those whom the Lord commends, who of themselves are nothing and can boast only of weakness. This is the heart of his argument, as 10:18 clearly shows.

His extraordinary ascent to heaven was certainly evidence of the Lord's commendation. This experience is to be compared to his "Damascus road" vision and calling. Both were granted to him by the Lord. He calls both "revelations." The first relates to his call and commission as an apostle, the second is a highly privileged confirmation of the Lord's commendation. Indeed, I would maintain that this journey to heaven is a higher and more privileged experience than that of the epiphany at his conversion. As Albert Schweitzer pointed out, all of the apostles had "seen the Lord," but as far as we have evidence, *only Paul* had been taken to heaven and told secrets he could not disclose.[84] It is precisely *because* he regarded this experience so highly that he is most careful and reticent in recounting it to the Corinthians. He does not want it to be taken as the same kind of boasting that characterized his opponents. At the same time he is eager to demonstrate that he is not the least bit inferior to the opponents.

My argument in this section of the chapter is that Paul's experience of ascent to Paradise is related to the ways he exercises authority in his churches. I have shown how he asserts that authority in various situations in his letters. It is his unwavering conviction that he "speaks for the Lord." That authority is based on his self-understanding as an apostle: an apostle whom the Lord has called; upon whom the power of Christ rests; whom the Lord, not men, has commended. In a crisis situation, such as that reflected in 2 Corinthians, when that very authority is called into question, he asserts it all the more, with a rigor unparalleled in any of his other letters. In this context his recounting of his ascent to heaven is his way of affirming in the boldest possible manner that he is the one commended by the Lord, that he is the one who must be heeded. He does indeed "boast" in his weakness in this chapter, but that very "weakness" came as a result of his highly privileged revelations (12:7). For Paul the issue is singular and clear cut--the opponents are of Satan, while he speaks and acts with the authority of Christ.

Last of All He Appeared to Me

Paul did not view his apostolic authority in a vacuum, but understood it in the context of his apostolic *mission*. Apostolic authority and mission must be seen hand in hand, together forming his apostolic self-understanding. After listing the appearances of the risen Christ to Cephas, to "the twelve," to James, and then to all the "apostles," he tells of his own selection:

> Last of all, as to one abnormally born, he appeared also to me. For I am the least of the apostles, actually not fit to be called an apostle, because I persecuted the church of God. But by the grace of God I am what I am, and his grace toward me was not in vain. On the contrary, *I worked harder than all of them, though it was not I, but God's grace in me.* Therefore whether it was I or they, this is what we preach and this is what you believe (1 Cor. 15:8-11).

Paul finds it important to stress that he and the other apostles preach the same message (15:1-4), and that together they form a single line of witnesses to the resurrection of Jesus. But even here, when he wants to stress this unity and continuity with the others, he actually separates himself from them. Christ appeared to him last. He is like an untimely birth. He is the least of the apostles, not even worthy to be one at all. All of this is self-deprecating. But at the same time, from another viewpoint, these very factors can be seen to underline the *special* position that he holds. He says he "worked harder than all the others," so the grace God extended to him was not ineffectual; then quickly adds that none of this was due to *him*, but to God who worked through him.[85] Paul understands his call and mission as an apostle as *sui generis*, different from the others. It is worth noting that 1 Cor. 15 is not a context in which he is defending himself as an apostle (in contrast to 1 Cor. 9), yet this same kind of tone still comes through. Paul sees his mission and role in the plan of God as special and important, separate and beyond that of any of the other leaders.

He sees himself as one called to a very particular mission. I pointed out previously how Rom. 1:3-4 offers a terse summary of Paul's essential message. The very next verse is a similarly formulaic statement regarding his mission:

38

> Through whom [Christ] we have received grace and apostleship for *the obedience of faith among all the Gentile nations* for the sake of his name.

This language is echoed in Rom. 15:18, which comes in the middle of one of the most basic treatments of his understanding of this mission:[86]

> For I will not dare to speak of anything except what Christ has accomplished *through me*, to win the *obedience of the Gentiles* ....

In Gal. 1:16 he says most directly that God called him through his grace and revealed his Son to him, "*in order that I might preach him among the Gentiles.*" He goes on to explain his understanding of the difference between his apostolic mission and that of Peter (and the others at Jerusalem):

> For the one who worked through Peter for the mission (*apostolēn*) to the circumcised, worked also through me for the *mission to the Gentiles* (2:8).

He claims that the others accepted this understanding of his work, which he relates back to his initial conversion and call. He would go to the Gentiles, the others to the Jews (2:9). He calls himself an "apostle to the Gentiles" (Rom. 11:13), and it is this fundamental mission which gives him his special role in the plan of God. These passages from Paul's own letters (in contrast to Acts), show how utterly *Jewish* the earliest Christian movement was. All of the Jerusalem apostles concentrate on the primary mission, the witness to Israel. This scheme makes no sense at all for the later movement and is only to be understood in the intensely apocalyptic times before the Jewish War and the fall of the Temple. As Johannes Munck has shown (though his book might have better been called, "Paul and the Salvation of All *Israel*" rather than "Mankind"), Paul understands his special role as apostle to the Gentiles as the key to the final events of the End. He presents his understanding of this eschatological plan in Rom. 9-11 and 15:7-33. God has not rejected his people Israel, even though, at the present time, only a few have joined the Messianic movement (11:1-5). This is in keeping with God's inscrutable ways. Through their rejection of Jesus as the Messiah, salvation is now being offered to the Gentiles, to make Israel jealous (11:11-12). It is all part of the secret plan of God, now revealed by Paul. He tells the Gentile believers:

> I want you to understand this mystery brethren, so you won't be conceited: a hardening has come upon part of Israel, *until the full number of the Gentiles come in*, and thus all Israel will be saved (11:25-26b).[87]

Paul understands that there is a certain select group of Gentiles that God has chosen and is calling to make up a new Israelite community (Gal. 6:16; Phil. 3:3). His preaching in the major cities of the empire, both east and west, is the means by which they are gathered together and prepared for their role in God's plan. When his work is completed he expects Israel as a whole to come to believe in Jesus as Messiah and Lord.

Paul develops this understanding of his Gentile mission through an interpretation of prophetic texts in the Hebrew Bible, particularly sections of deutero-Isaiah. This is a major factor in understanding the dynamics of Paul's apostolic consciousness--he literally *finds himself and his apostolic mission* in these texts of sacred Scripture. Isa. 49:1-6 (LXX) is perhaps the single most significant text. I have put the phrases and terms in italics which Paul may have understood to refer to his own ministry:

> Listen to me, O coastlands,
> and hearken you *Gentiles*;
> *After a long time it will happen,*
> says the Lord.
> *From my mother's womb he has called my name.*
> And he has made my *mouth a sharp sword*,
> and he has hidden me, under the shadow of his hand;
> He has made me as a choice shaft,
> and he has hidden me in his quiver.
> And he said to me, "You are *my servant*, O Israel,
> and *in you I will be glorified*."
> Then I said, "*I have labored in vain*,
> therefore this is *my judgment with the Lord*,
> And now, thus says the Lord that
> formed me *from the womb to be his own servant*,
> *to gather Jacob to him and Israel*.
> I shall be gathered and glorified before the Lord,
> *and God shall be my strength*.
> And he said to me, "It is a great thing
> for you to be called *my servant*,
> *to establish the tribes of Jacob*,
> *and to recover the dispersion of Israel*.
> Behold, I have given you *for a covenant* of a race,
> for a *light of the Gentiles*,
> *that you should be for salvation*,
> *to the ends of the earth*.

Paul directly quotes this chapter in 2 Cor. 6:2. He alludes to it in Gal. 1:15 when speaking of his call before his birth, and again in Phil. 2:16 when he contemplates the final outcome of his work. In Rom. 15:21, where he defends his special mission to the Gentiles, he quotes from Isa. 52:15, a closely related section of deutero-Isaiah. More significant than these allusions or direct quotations is the way in which Paul's general understanding of his role corresponds so closely to the thematic thought-world of such texts. He, like the Hebrew prophets, is called by God at a crucial moment of history. The language he uses to describe this call in Gal. 1:15 seems to echo Jeremiah's commission:

> Before I formed you in the womb
> I knew you,
> and *before you were born* I
> consecrated you;
> *I appointed you a prophet to the nations* (Jer. 1:5).

Paul writes of his own commission:

> But when he who had *set me apart before my birth*, and had
> called me through his grace, was pleased to reveal his Son to me,
> so that I might *preach him among the Gentile nations*, I did not
> consult with flesh and blood . . . Gal. 1:15)

Jeremiah's authority to "destroy" and "build" (Jer. 1:10) might well lie behind Paul's formulaic language in 2 Cor. 10:8 and 13:10. Paul's extreme statement that he wished he could be cursed by God in order to save Israel (Rom. 9:1-3) corresponds to Moses' prayer in Exodus 32:30-34 where he asks that he be destroyed rather than the nation of Israel. Paul directly contrasts his ministry with that of Moses in 2 Cor. 3. He sees himself as doing a greater work. He seems to identify his situation with that of Elijah: the lone and faithful servant of God, rejected by all (Rom. 11:2-6). My point is that Paul pictures his role in the plan of God in the same language as that used for the greatest figures of Israel's past. In the case of the deutero-Isaiah material, I think he goes even further. He actually sees himself as fulfilling the role of the "Servant" who brings Israel back to God through a ministry to the Gentile nations. This is not to deny that he may have seen Jesus also as such a servant.[88] He says in Rom. 15:8 that "Christ became a servant to the circumcised . . . *in order that* the Gentiles might glorify God." This is the key to Paul's thinking. Both Jesus' and Peter's preaching to Jews was a *ministry of hardening*, which would in turn *lead to* his own ministry to the Gentiles, which would then finally bring about the salvation of Israel (Rom. 11:7). Paul's mission and role are therefore absolutely central to the sequence of this plan of God. Paul recognizes the greatness of the task he has been given. In Rom. 11:13, after explaining the basic outline of the plan, he says, "Inasmuch as I am an apostle to the Gentiles, I *exalt my ministry*." Later, in chapter 15, he says he has written "boldly" (v.15) to them, explaining:

> *In* Christ Jesus, then, I have reason to boast of my work for God.
> For I will not dare to speak of anything except *what Christ has*
> *worked through me, to win obedience from the Gentiles* . . . (15:17-
> 18).

This is the same kind of language he uses in 2 Cor. 10-13 as we have seen. Paul's "modesty" in Christ does not mean that he lacks any appreciation for the importance of his role in God's plan. On the contrary, his assertion that his work is from and through Christ makes it all the more significant. His calling was special and he receives spiritual power from Christ himself to carry out the work.

In Romans 15:7-29 he sets forth his *modus operandi*. He has been called as a "priestly servant" (*leitourgon*) of Jesus Christ to the Gentile nations, in the priestly service (*hierougounta*) of the Gospel of God, *so that* the offering (*prosphora*) of the Gentiles" may be acceptable (15:16). His collection from the Gentiles churches, which he was preparing to take to Jerusalem, is an embodiment of that priestly service (v. 27).[89]. He likely has in mind Isa. 2:2-4 and 60:5-9, where the Gentile nations are to flow into Jerusalem bearing gifts from all nations of the world. He feels that this offering from his churches in Macedonia, Achaia, and Asia is a vital sign of the validity of his mission (Rom. 15:27; 2 Cor. 9:12-15). At the time he writes the letter to Rome, he has finished his work in the East (15:19-23), and after the trip to Jerusalem with the funds he has raised, plans to move on to the West, via Rome, to Spain; and then his commission will be completed (15:24-29). This extraordinary sense of itinerary illustrates just how concretely he understands his role in God's eschatological plan. He is headed for unknown regions, fired by the vision of deutero-Isaiah, that "those who have never heard" shall be told (Isa. 52:15; Rom. 15:21).

Closely tied to this understanding of mission is Paul's idea about suffering in behalf of his congregations.[90] His model here is Jesus, but he seems to be drawing as well, from themes in deutero-Isaiah. Since all believers are "in Christ," and the paradigms of suffering/glory and weakness/power lie at the center of his theology of the cross, *all* "share abundantly in Christ's sufferings" (2 Cor. 1:3-7). This is related to his idea of imitation. He tells the Thessalonians that they "became imitators of us and of the Lord" because they faced great affliction (1 Thess. 1:5; cf. 2:15). But there is a sense in which Paul's sufferings are different. He represents Christ, present to his churches, and like Christ he suffers on their behalf.

In the fragments of 2 Cor. 2:14-6:13, 7:2-4, Paul gives his most profound description of his "ministry." One should note carefully his use of the first and second person in this section. I am convinced that when he uses the plural "we" he is speaking of his own particular work as an apostle. He has his special role in mind, not the ministry in general.[91] He is the aroma of Christ to God, the one through whom the world is being divided into two classes, those who are being saved and those who are perishing (2:15-16). He has received his commission from God and "speaks in Christ" (2:17). His message is that Jesus is Lord, and he is *their servant*, because of Jesus (4:5). The catalogue of sufferings (4:8-9) is described as "carrying in the body *the death of Jesus*" which leads to life for them (4:10-12). All this is "for your sake" he tells them (4:15). He has been given a "work of reconciliation" so that God makes his appeal *through him to them* (5:18-20). He is Christ's "ambassador" (5:20). The commendation of his ministry is his abundant sufferings (6:4-10). This latter passage is quite similar to 11:23-29, where he also lists his trials and sufferings, speaking as a "fool." The same contrast between Paul and the community is found in 1 Cor. 4:8-13, where his irony expresses a judgmental tone. As an apostle he is "last of all" like one "sentenced to death," a "spectacle" (*theatron*) before men and angels (4:9).[92] He recounts his many sufferings (4:11-13), describing himself as the "refuse of the world," and the "offscouring of all things."[93] Paul concludes his heated letter to the Galatians with the sharp declaration, "From now on let no one bother me, I bear on my body the marks (*stigmata*) of Jesus!" (6:17). Whatever he means by "marks," he appears to have in mind some type of suffering which he relates to Jesus' own.[94] His most explicit statement is in Phillippians, where he is contemplating his possible death (1:19-26). He tells them: "Even if I am to be poured out upon the sacrificial offering of your faith, I am glad and rejoice with you all." The language is difficult to interpret, but he appears to picture himself as a sacrificial priest who will offer their faith as a gift (cf. Rom. 15:16, 27), crowned with the pouring out of his own blood over it.[95] In 3:8 he says that he has suffered "the loss of all things" for the sake of Christ. He is like Jesus, who "emptied himself" and gave up all he had (2:7). But he expects more than suffering, he expects to die like Christ as well:

> I may know him and the power of his resurrection, and may *share his sufferings*, becoming *like him in his death*, that if possible I may attain the resurrection from the dead (3:10-11).

The way he describes the resurrection in this verse is unusual. Rather than the standard phrase "*anastasis tōn vekrōn*," He uses *ei pōs* with the verb, the prefix *ex* with *anastasis* followed by the preposition *ek* with *nekrōn*. The tone of the verse is also different, as if Paul is speaking of something other than the general hope of resurrection of the dead at Jesus' coming. Albert Schweitzer has argued that Paul has in mind a special and immediate translation to heaven, like that of Enoch or Elijah in Jewish tradition.[96] If he dies, he will "depart to be with Christ," he says (Phil. 1:23). This is not something he expected for other believers who had died, as he makes clear in 1 Thess. 4:13-18; 1 Cor. 15). The "dead in Christ" will *rise to meet Christ in the air* at his return. Paul's language in Phil. 1:23 and 3:11-12 is difficult to reconcile with this more general hope. There is the language from 2 Cor. 5:1-10 which describes death as being "absent from the body" and "at home with the Lord," which many would take, along with Phil. 1:23, as evidence for Paul having shifted his thinking on this question of the "state of the dead."[97] I think this is highly unlikely. The language of 2 Cor. 5:6-8 can and likely does refer to the Parousia (v.10); whereas Phil. 1:23 can *only* refer to Paul's death. Schweitzer's proposal seems to make the best sense. It fits well with his overall notion of being called for a high mission. Paul sees himself after deutero-Isaiah's model of a "suffering servant." Isa. 49:7 speaks of one whom God has chosen as "deeply despised" and "abhorred by the nations." He quotes Isa. 49:8 in 2 Cor. 6:2, and alludes to the chapter in two other places, as we have seen (Gal. 1:15; Phil. 2:16); while vv. 1-6 describe his mission in detail. He quotes Isa. 52:13 and applies it to his ministry in Rom.

43

15:21, and the very next verse, Isa. 52:14, speaks of the servant "marred beyond human semblance." There can be little doubt that Paul has worked through this section of Isaiah and it has influenced his understanding of his role. This whole matter is complicated by two factors. Paul's model is Jesus, so the language he applies to himself from deutero-Isaiah regarding suffering he may well have also applied to Jesus. He is, in turn, the model for the community, so even if he speaks of his suffering *for them*, they too are to learn to follow him in this regard. But neither of these factors diminishes the obvious way he does understand his apostleship as a special call to bear suffering. And this role is part of his eschatological mission.

Hans Windisch, in his valuable study *Paulus und Christus*, has shown how similar Paul and Jesus are, in the portrayal in Acts, as well as in Paul's own letters. He argues that both fit the type of the *theios anēr*, that both are prophet, apostle, pneumatic, teacher, scribe, servant and mystagogue. Indeed, Paul can be seen as "greater" than Jesus in that he is sent to all nations, while Jesus went only to Israel. There is some truth to this. Paul is called to be God's servant to the Gentiles, but this is Christ's service, carried out through his power. But the "slippage" inherent in Paul's language is the problem. Certainly for Paul, Jesus is Lord, he is the Son of God, the suffering one, the one who has been exalted to God's throne with all power and glory. Yet his message is that he, and all believers, are destined to rule, are the Sons of God, must also suffer in this present time, but will be glorified and exalted at the End. So we have Christ, Paul and his communities. The same language, with various nuances, can be applied to all. Still, in for the present historical working out of God's plan, Paul's special identity does stand apart. His task is different from Jesus' (Rom. 15:8-12). Indeed, it was Jesus' ministry that really prepared the way for his own role in bringing about the final events of history. Both Jesus and Paul are servants and agents in the plan (1 Cor. 15:28). God sent forth his Son. He commissions Paul. Yet, at root, Paul is theocentric. The beginning and end of God's purposes belong to God alone. He expresses this most eloquently in Rom. 11:33-36. Still, as apostle to the Gentiles, Paul's work is more important than, and far surpasses that, of even the greatest figures of Israel's history, or of any of the other apostles. As Munck pointed out, he has been appointed by God to fill the *key* position in the last great drama of salvation.[98]

Conclusions

The question of how Paul evaluated his ascent to Paradise cannot be settled from the internal evidence of his letters alone. We only know of it from a single passage, the context of which is easily one of the most difficult sections of the Pauline corpus. I see nothing in this context, nor in the way he reports the experience, that indicates he disparaged such an experience. On the contrary, I have argued that a careful reading of 2 Cor. 10-13 shows that he highly valued it. I have shown that such a vision of heavenly glory would have closely correlated with what I argue is at the core of his message, namely, his expectation of the glorification of the many Sons of God. At the same time I have argued that his understanding of his apostolic authority and special mission fits well with his many "visions and revelations" of the Lord, all of which were highly privileged, but especially his ascent to Paradise. This last point is further supported from what we know of the general phenomena of the journey to heaven in its wider Greco-Roman/Jewish context. To this I turn in the next chapter.

NOTES TO CHAPTER TWO

1. Albert Schweitzer's *Mysticism* remains the classic study arguing that Paul's theology develops from his understanding of 'being in Christ'. There is also the important study of Adolf Deismann on Paul as the "Christ-mystic' (*Paul: A Study in Social and Religious History*, 2d ed. [New York: Harper & Row, 1926]). Rudolf Bultmann (*Theology of the New Testament* [New York: Charles Scribner's Sons, 1951], 1: 270-352) certainly offers the most representative presentation of the position that 'justification by faith' is the heart of Paul's thought. Important to the subsequent discussion are Krister Stendahl, "The Apostle Paul and the Introspective Conscience of the West," *HTR* 56 (1963): 199-215 and Ernst Käsemann, "Justification and Salvation History," *Perspectives on Paul* (Philadelphia: Fortress Press, 1971), pp. 60-78. See also the helpful orientation and collection of essays by Wayne Meeks (*The Writings of St. Paul* [New York: W. W. Norton, 1972], pp. 361-444).

2. E. P. Sanders, *Paul and Palestinian Judaism: A Comparison of Patterns of Religion* (Philadelphia: Fortress Press, 1977), pp. 431-523. I mention Sanders' work in particular here because I consider this section of his book to be the best recent summary of the major issues in the field of Pauline studies. I am not intending to evaluate here his project in the book as a whole, which I leave to those better trained in the Jewish materials (See Neusner's essay review in *HR* 18 [1978]: 177-91.) Sanders seems to be one of the few contemporary N.T. scholars who is willing to take seriously the implications of Schweitzer's work, see his comments on "relevance" in *Paul and Palestinian Judaism*, pp. 520-523. In contrast, J. Christian Beker (and so many others), despite all this talk about a "literal" understanding of Paul's apocalyptic, never *really* take Paul seriously as a Jew, and thus a participant in the apocalyptic dramas of the decades before 70 C.E.; see *Paul the Apostle* (Philadelphia: Fortress Press, 1980), but especially his *Paul's Apocalyptic Gospel* (Philadelphia: Fortress Press, 1982) pp. 79-121.

3. Morton Smith's recent article, "Salvation in the Gospels, Paul, and the Magical Papyri," *Helios* 13 (1986): 63-74, is one of the few that focuses

directly on the question.

4. Sanders' important and long overdue critique of the way most Christian scholars have misunderstood forms of ancient Judaism as legalistic, in contrast to Paul's ideas about grace and freedom, might lead one to assume that the most basic question to ask about a religious system is how one "gets in and stays in." The very agenda then gets set by these Christians who have made this legalism/grace question *the* issue. Sanders explains that he purposely limited his investigation of Paul to this particular issue in this particular study, see *Paul, the Law, and the Jewish People*, pp. 3-15.

5. Sanders, *Paul*, pp. 441-42.

6. See Johannes Munck, *Christ and Israel: An Interpretation of Romans 9-11* trans. (Philadelphia: Fortress Press, 1967), pp. 107-8. Cf. 1 Pet. 1:20 and *prognosis* in Acts 2:23 and 1 Pet. 1:2.

7. On the special vocabulary and complexities of 1 Cor. 1:18-2:16 see Ulrich Wilckens, *Weisheit und Torheit: eine exegetisch-religionsgeschichtlich Untersuchung zu 1 Kor 1 und 2* (Tübingen: J. C. B. Mohr, 1959) and Birger A. Pearson, *The Pneumatikos-Psychikos Terminology* (Missoula: Scholars Press, 1973).

8. Cf. Rom. 16:25. Also the deutero-Pauline materials should be noted: Eph. 3:9, 11; Col. 1:26; the use of *katabolē* in Eph. 1:4 (which is found in several places in the New Testament: Matt. 25:34; Luke 11:50; 1 Pet. 1:20; Rev. 13:8; 17:8.

9. He also uses *mustērion* for the historical purpose of God in initiating his Gentile mission and its function for the salvation of Israel (Rom. 11:25-56; 16:25-26). Cf. 1 Cor. 4:1; 13:2; 14:2 and the deutero-Pauline materials (Eph. 1:19; 3:3-9; 6:19; Col. 1:26-27; 2:2; 4:3). The best discussion of this concept of "mystery" in Paul and in the wider context of religions of the period is Morton Smith, *Clement of Alexandria and a Secret Gospel of Mark* (Cambridge: Harvard University Press, 1973), pp. 178ff.

10. Martin Dibelius, *Die Geisterwelt im Glauben des Paulus* (Göttingen: Vandenhoech & Ruprecht, 1909), pp. 90-96 and Hans Bietenhard, *Die himmlische Welt im Urchristentum und Spätjudentum* (Tübingen: J. C. B. Mohr, 1951) are still the best on this subject. I think Paul's other references to the "principalities and powers" (especially 1 Cor. 15:24) makes it unlikely that he has in mind human civil authorities (see Rom. 13:1) in this passage. Paul is thinking in terms of a cosmic battle, of the conquering of death itself, and it is only in this context that his notion of glorification makes sense.

11. I cannot agree here with Erhardt Güttgemanns (*Der leidende Apostel und sein Herr: Studien zur paulinischen Christologie* [Göttingen: Vandenhoeck & Ruprecht, 1966], pp. 240-47) that Phil. 3:20-21 is a pre-Pauline hymn. See the

discussion and critique of this position by Robert H. Grundry, *Soma in Biblical Theology with Emphasis on Pauline Anthropology* (Cambridge: University Press, 1976), pp. 177-83.

12. Dieter Georgi represents one of the best treatments of the problems involved; see his study, *Die Gegner des Paulus im 2. Korintherbrief: Studien zur religiösen Propaganda in der Spätantike* (Neukirchen-Vluyn: Neukirchener Verlag, 1964), pp. 258-89.

13. I will deal with 2 Cor 4:16-5:1-10 below.

14. See Robin Scroggs, *The Last Adam: A Study in Pauline Anthropology* (Philadelphia: Fortress Press, 1966), pp. 97-100, who discusses these passages and evaluates the positions of Friedrich Eltester (*Eikon im Neuen Testament* [Berlin: A. Töpelmann, 1958]) and Jacob Jervell (*Imago Dei* [Göttingen: Vandenhoeck & Ruprecht, 1960]).

15. See Col. 1:18 and Rev. 1:5. See the rather striking parallel thought in Heb. 2:10 where God is bringing "many sons into glory," of whom Jesus is the first.

16. *klēromeo* occurs in 1 Cor. 6:9,10; 15:50; Gal. 4:30; 5:21; *klēronomia* once in Gal. 3:18. *klēronomos* occurs in Rom. 4:13, 14; 8:17; Gal. 3:29; 4:1,7. Cf. Eph. 1:11,14,18; Col. 3:24.

17. See Bruce M. Metzger, *A Textual Commentary on the Greek New Testament* (New York: United Bible Societies, 1971), p. 517.

18. Morton Smith comments on this point in a note to me: "That believers already have the 'spirit of sonship' and are 'sons of God,' was evidently an important factor in Paul's preaching and conversions (to judge from the reactions of his converts in 1 and 2 Cor. and his warnings in Gal. 5 and the end of Phil., cf. 2 Thess. 2:2). It would have been, for it distinguished his religion from the dismal 'pie in the sky' asceticism of later Paulinism, whether whether monastic or puritanical. Paul's world is not *exclusively* a vale of tears, nor is his reward *wholly* future. He both carries about the death of Christ in his body and manifests the glory of Christ in his spirit and his gospel *now*." I agree wholly.

19. Rom. 1:6-7; 8:28; 9:24; 1 Cor. 1:2, 9, 24; Gal. 1:6; 5:8; 1 Thess. 2:12; 4:7; 5:24; Phil. 3:14.

20. The scholarly discussion of this hymn has been extensive. It is generally agreed that the verses contain pre-Pauline material. For an extensive bibliography on the passage see Ralph P. Martin, *Carmen Christi: Philippians ii. 5-11 in Recent Interpretation and in the Setting of Early Christian Worship*, published in an enlarged 2d ed. (Grand Rapids: Eerdmans, 1983).

21. "The Problem of Pre-Existence in Phil. 2:6-11," *JBL* 86 (1967): 141-153.

22. I say cautiously because I realize the complicated mythology this hymn reflects. See the argument of Morton Smith that the hymn represents the second half of an "Enoch myth" in *Clement of Alexandria*, pp. 245-6. Still, I find it doubtful that Paul sees Jesus as a pre-existent divine heavenly figure here or elsewhere. See the further discussion of J. Murphy-O'Conner, "Christological Anthropology in Phil. 2:6-11," *RB* 83 (1976): 25-50, and in general, James D. G. Dunn, *Christology in the Making* (Philadelphia: Westminster, 1980).

23. For an excellent survey of the history of interpretation regarding this group who denied the resurrection, as well as an extensive bibliography, see Bernhard Spörlein, *Die Leugnung der Auferstehung* (Regensburg: Verlag Friedrich Pustet, 1971).

24. This is Schweitzer's position (*Mysticism*, p. 93). One problem with this view is that it does not take the 1 Cor. letter as a whole, dealing with sections such as 3:1-4; 4:8-13; 10:1-12; 12-14, which might reflect a general problem with some kind of "over-realized" eschatology. Still new consideration has been given to the possibility of an Epicurean position behind some of the polemics of the N.T. (See Jerome H. Neyrey, "The Form and Background of the Polemic in 2 Peter," *JBL* 99 [1980]: 407-31). The real strength of this position is that it seems to best fit Paul's argument in 15:29-34, while the other interpretations appear to make little sense here.

25. See Spörlein, *Leugnung*, pp. 171-88 for the variations on this position. For arguments see Archibald Robertson and Alfred Plummer, *I Corinthians* 2d ed. (Edinburgh: T & T Clark, 1914), pp. 345-48.

26. Walter Schmithals, *Gnosticism in Corinth: An Investigation of the Letters to the Corinthians* (Nashville: Abingdon Press, 1971), pp. 155-59 argues that Paul misunderstood his opponents.

27. Paul probably knew of various speculations among Jewish circles regarding a Primal Man (*Urmensch*). This has been extensively investigated. See the summary of Robert Jewett, *Paul's Anthropological Terms: A Study of Their Use in Conflict Settings* (Leiden: E. J. Brill, 1971), pp. 230-36 and the discussion of Robin Scroggs, *The Last Adam*, pp. 97-100.

28. The studies of this passage are many. See Ernst Käsemann, *Commentary on Romans* (Eerdmans: Grand Rapids, 1980), pp. 4-5 for a bibliography.

29. This interpretation hinges on the use of *epeita/eita* (vv. 23-24) and whether the verbs of v. 24 with the double use of *hotan* refer to what is to be accomplished in a time period between the Parousia and what he calls *to telos* I would translate *hotan katargēsē* as "*after* destroying." On this interpretation see Schweitzer, *Mysticism*, pp. 75-100. For a full-scale study of the ques-

tion see H. A. Wilcke, *Das Problem eines messianischen Zwischenreiches bei Paulus* (Zurich: Zwingli Verlag, 1951).

30. Scroggs, *Last Adam*, pp. 92-112. Also C. K. Barrett, *From First Adam to Last: A Study in Pauline Theology* (New York: Charles Scribner's Sons, 1962), pp. 92-119 and Egon Brandenburger, *Adam und Christus* (Neukirchen: Neukirchen Verlag, 1962).

31. How this rather "Jewish" line of exegesis was continued, especially in Asia Minor by Theophilus, see Robert M. Grant, "Jewish Christianity at Antioch in the Second Century," *RSR* 60 (1972): 97-108 and my article, "The Theology of Redemption of Theophilus of Antioch," *RQ* 18 (1975): 159-171 and in general, Jean Daniélou, *Jewish Christianity*, passim.

32. For standard treatments see Johannes Munck, *Paul and the Salvation of Mankind* (Richmond: John Knox Press, 1959), pp. 11-35; W. D. Davies, *Paul and Rabbinic Judaism*, 3d ed. (London: S. P. C. K., 1970), pp. 66-68; H. J. Schoeps *Paul: The Theology of the Apostle in the Light of Jewish Religious History* (Philadelphia: Westminster Press, 1959), pp. 53-59; Günther Bornkamm, *Paul* (New York: Harper and Row, 1971), pp. 13-30.

33. See the discussion of Bornkamm, *Paul*, pp. 19-22.

34. C. K. Barrett, *The Second Epistle to the Corinthians* (New York: Harper and Row, 1973), p. 34. See also Davies, *Paul*, pp. 197-98. In contrast note the approach of Schoeps, *Paul*, pp. 74-78, who takes seriously the kind of historical situation in which claims to visions and revelations were evaluated and disputed.

35. See the helpful discussion of Hans Dieter Betz on this whole issue, *Galatians* (Philadelphia: Fortress Press, 1979), pp. 64-66.

36. John Howard Schütz, *Paul and the Anatomy of Apostolic Authority* (Cambridge: University Press, 1975). Also quite valuable is a subsequent study by Bengt Holmberg, *Paul and Power: The Structure of Authority in the Primitive Church as Reflected in the Pauline Epistles* (Philadelphia: Fortress Press, 1978).

37. See the discussion of Schütz, *Anatomy of Apostolic Authority*, p. 30.

38. The textual variants *nēpioi/ēioi* are impossible to resolve. *ēpioi* seems to fit the context best though it only occurs elsewhere in 2 Tim. 2:24. See Metzger, *Textual Commentary*, pp. 629-30 for a discussion.

39. Schütz, *Anatomy of Apostolic Authority*, p. 19.

40. Ibid., p. 13

41. See Reitzenstein, *Hellenistic Mystery-Religions*, pp. 461-64, on this difficult passage. Compare 1 Tim. 1:20.

42. For example, *1 Clement* 42.

43. See the treatments of Hans Conzelmann, *First Corinthians* (Philadelphia: Fortress Press, 1975), pp. 181-91 and Elisabeth Schüssler Fiorenza, *In Memory of Her: A Feminist Theological Reconstruction of Christian Origins* (New York: Crossroad, 1983), pp. 226-33.

44. Cf. 1 Cor. 11:23; 15:3 and his use of the verb *paradidomi* for a received unit of tradition officially handed on to his churches. Chapter 11:2 reflects a rather different case. Here Paul is discussing detailed matters of dress, hair style and regulations for prayer (v. 16), and he appeals to his *own* traditions as authority. Cf. 1 Thess. 4:1-2, 8.

45. There is a textual question as to whether one is to read *agnoeitai* or the imperative *agnoeito*, which is also well supported. See Metzger, *Textual Commentary*, p. 566. The imperative might be seen to carry more of a sense of cursing rather than mere declaration. Compare Gal. 1:8-9; 5:10; 6:17 and Betz's treatment of these passages (*Galatians*, pp. 50-52, 266-70, 223-25). Also compare 1 Cor. 16:22.

46. Probably reflecting the tradition now preserved in Mark 10:2-12 and Q (Matt. 5:31-32; Luke 16:18).

47. It is used for persons in authority who issues orders and directives. In 1 Cor. 9:14 it occurs in another logion of Jesus which Paul quotes. He uses it in Gal. 3:19 for the giving of the 10 commandments! Elsewhere in the N.T.: Claudius commanding the Jews to leave Rome (Acts 18:2); Felix 's directive regarding Paul's arrest (Acts 24:23); a master commanding a servant (Luke 17:9-10); Jesus commissioning the 12 apostles (Matt. 10:5).

48. See Schütz, *Anatomy of Apostolic Authority*, pp. 12-14. The *auctor* can offer reasons for his will, though he need not do so.

49. For the best analysis of this language see Betz, *Galatians*, pp. 47-54, 130-31, 266-70.

50. Ibid., pp. 50-52, Betz has an excursus on this curse.

51. Schütz, *Anatomy of Apostolic Authority*, pp. 204-5.

52. In addition to the standard commentaries see Josef Zmijewski, *Der Stil der paulinischen "Narrenrede": Analyse der Sprachgestaltung in 2 Kor 11, 1-12,10* (Cologne: Peter Hanstein Verlag, 1978); and especially Hans Dieter

Betz, *Der Apostel Paulus und die sokratische Tradition: Eine exegetische Unter-suchung zu seiner "Apologie" 2 Korinther 10-13* (Tübingen: J. C. B. Mohr, 1972).

53. Two of the best reviews of the research are E. Earle Ellis, "Paul and His Opponents," *Christianity, Judaism and Other Greco-Roman Cults,* ed. Jacob Neusner, 4 vols. (Leiden: E. J. Brill, 1975), 2: 264-98 and Dieter Georgi, *Die Gegner des Paulus,* pp. 1-29. In addition to the standard commentaries, some of the more important studies are: F. C. Baur, "Die Christus-partei in der Korinthischen Gemeinde," *TZ* 4 (1831): 61-82; Richard Reitzenstein, *Hellenistic Mystery-Religions,* pp. 426-500; Ernst Käsemann, "Die Legitimität des Apostles, *ZNTW* 41 (1942): 33-71; Schoeps, *Paul,* pp. 74-87; Munck, *Paul and the Salvation of Mankind,* pp. 168-95; Gerhard Friedrich, "Die Gegner des Paulus im zweiten Korintherbrief," *Abraham unser Vater* (Leiden: E. J. Brill, 1963), pp. 181-215; D. W. Oostendorp, *Another Jesus: A Gospel of Jewish-Christian Superiority in II Corinthians* (Kampen: J. H. Kok;, 1967); Schmithals, *Gnosticism in Corinth* (Nashville: Abingdon Press, 1971); C. K. Barrett, "Paul's Opponents in II Corinthians," *NTS* 17 (1971):233-54.

54. John J. Gunther, *St. Paul's Opponents and their Background: A study of Apocalyptic and Jewish Sectarian Teachings* (Leiden: E. J. Brill, 1973), p. 1.

55. Kasemann ("Die Legitimität"), while not sharing the view of Bauer and Schoeps that the opponents are "non-pneumatic" Judaizers, has argued that the "superlative apostles" (11:5; 12:11) are, nonetheless, the Jerusalem apostles, from whom these opponents at Corinth claimed authorization. This has also been accepted by Barrett, "Paul's Opponents," pp. 242-44.

56. This is Schoep's summary of *Homily* 17:14-19 (*Paul,* p. 83).

57. See the rigorous criticism of Schmithals (*Gnosticism in Corinth,* pp. 117-20) who concludes: "The thesis that in his letters to Corinth Paul is dealing with Judaizers is to be abandoned without reservation, in whatever form and with whatever dilution it may be proposed." (p. 120). He is most critical of Baur, but also makes reference to Windisch, Lietzmann, Kümmel and Käsemann as holding modified forms of a 'Judaizing' view. For further criticism and argument see Friedrich, "Die Gegner," pp. 192-96; Georgi, *Gegner,* pp. 7-16; Munck, *Paul,* pp. 168-95.

58. This is one of the major contributions of Betz's extensive study, *Paulus und die sokratische Tradition.* On this point see Schmithals, *Gnosticism,* pp. 209-11 (against Windisch and Schoeps).

59. *Gnosticism in Corinth,* pp. 188-89; 209-10.

60. This proposal has been quite influential has been accepted by Gunther Bornkamm ("The History of the Origin of the So-called Second Letter to the Corinthians," *NTS* 8 [1961]: 258-64) and Friedrich ("Die Gegner") among many others.

61. Helmut Koester ("Gnomai Diaphoroi," *HTR* 58 [1965]: 279-318) finds here one of his "trajectories" through early Christianity. This "divine man" Christology Paul faces at Corinth as similar to one which Mark opposed, and the triumph of this "heresy" can now be seen in the theology of Luke-Acts. For an very different interpretation of Mark's "Christology" see Jonathan Z. Smith, "Good News is No News," *Map is Not Territory* (Leiden: E. J. Brill, 1978), pp. 190-207.

62. For his evaluation and criticism of Georgi's work, see *Gnosticism*, pp. 287-93. After quoting Bornkamm's summary of 'Georgi's characterization of the false apostles, he says, "In essence I am able to agree with this throughout, ... In fact everything does argue for this view that the false apostles in Corinth are to be reckoned as belonging to this type of traveling Pneumatics." (p. 290).

63. Schmithal's case on this point is not finally convincing. See Barrett, *Second Corinthians*, pp. 5-30; Friedrich, "Die Gegner"; Oostendorp, *Another Jesus*, pp. 1-5; Munck, *Paul and the Salvation of Mankind*, pp. 168-71.

64. I think that Georgi has satisfactorily demonstrated this point, *Gegner*, pp. 51-82.

65. "Paul and his Opponents," pp. 297-98; italics are mine.

66. *Second Corinthians*, p. 34.

67. *Paul*, pp. 74-77. Cf. Käsemann, "Die Legitimitat," pp. 69-70.

68. *Paul*, pp. 87, 196-97.

69. James G. Dunn, *Jesus and the Spirit* (Philadelphia: Westminster, 1975), p. 213-216, 339.

70. Ibid., p. 277

71. "The Limits of Ecstasy: An Exegesis of 2 Corinthians 12:1-10," *Current Issues in Biblical and Patristic Interpretation*, ed. Gerald F. Hawthorne (Grand Rapids: Eerdmans, 1975), pp. 259-66.

72. "'Paul the Visionary': The Setting and Significance of the Rapture to Paradise in II Corinthians XII. 1-10," *NTS* 25 (1978): 204-220, and his later book, *Paradise Now and Not Yet* (Cambridge: Cambridge University Press, 1981), pp. 71-85.

73. "Visions, Revelations, and Ministry," which I noted previously. See Helmut Saake, "Paulus als Ekstatiker: Pneumatalogische Beobachtungen zu 2 Kor. xii 1-10," *NovT* 15 (1973): 153-60.

74. See Alfred Plummer, *Second Corinthians* (Edinburgh: T. & T. Clark, 1915), pp. 269-385 for a detailed treatment of the style and tone of this section of the letter, and always, Windisch, *Der Zweite Korintherbrief*, 9th ed. (Göttingen: Vandenhoeck & Ruprecht, 1924), pp. 365-81.

75. Compare Gal. 5:10-12, another extreme situation, where Paul expresses confidence that the community will take his view, while the enemy will "bear his judgment." How Paul feels about such enemies is well expressed in 1 Thess. 2:16, "God's wrath has come upon them at last!"

76. See his *Clement of Alexandria*, pp. 231ff. I have already mentioned the important treatment of Reitzenstein on this passage (*Hellenistic Mystery-Religions*), pp. 462ff.

77. Here I have restricted myself to the evidence in 2 Cor. 10-13. Some of the same issues are certainly present in 2:14-6:13 and elsewhere, including sections of 1 Cor. My purpose here is not to identify the theological stance of the opponents so much as to ask how the account of Paul's ascent functions in his defense.

78. Betz (*Paulus und sokratische Tradition*) represents the best full-scale discussion of the form of Paul's apology, relating it to elements in a Socratic tradition of making such defenses. His argument is most impressive, though he has been faulted with trying to "subordinate everything in these four chapters to this single line of interpretation" (Lincoln, "Paul the Visionary," p. 206). See Albert Henrichs review of Betz in *JBL* 94 (1975): 310-14, for further observations and qualifications.

79. I will deal with the specific elements of the experience in the final chapter. Betz (*Paulus und sokratische Tradition*, pp. 89-100) considers 12:2-4 and 7b-10 as two parodies. Paul tells of a vision, but reveals no revelatory word, he recounts a miracle story, but with no miracle. He maintains that this literary form diminishes, if not eliminates, the autobiographical value of the story. I can not agree with Betz here. The two reports are tightly connected, with the "thorn in the flesh" coming as a direct result of the exalted vision. The element of secrecy is just what we expect from magical materials telling of experiences of this sort (see my following chapter). That Paul's request for release or healing was *not* granted is the key to his whole argument in 11:30-12:11. The ascent for him, *becomes*, ironically, an experience of weakness. For a different, but related, critique of Betz's point here see Lincoln, "Paul the Visionary," pp. 209-10.

80. On this point see Plummer, *II Corinthians*, pp. 347-48.

81. See the many studies listed by Bruce Metzger, *Index to Periodical Literature on the Apostle Paul* (Grand Rapids: Eerdmans, 1960), pp. 15-16. More recently, Robert M. Price, "Punished in Paradise (An Exegetical Theory of II

THINGS UNUTTERABLE:PAUL'S ASCENT TO PARADISE

Corinthians 12:1-10)," *JSNT* 7 (1980): 33-40.

82. On this "bescheidenheitsstil" see Hans Windisch, *Der Zweite Korintherbrief*, pp. 369-70; Betz, *Paulus und sokratische Tradition*, pp. 91, 95; and the citations in *Str-B* 4:530-31.

83. I am taking the genitive here (*kuriou*--v.1) as subjective. See Plummer, *II Corinthians*, pp. 338.

84. Schweitzer, *Mysticism of Paul*, p. 137. This is also the view of Reitzenstein, *Hellenistic Mystery-Religions*, pp. 469-71. Such an evaluation would be strongly denied by most New Testament scholars, unfortunately, I would say, for theological reasons. As the following chapter will show, in its Greco-Roman context, this kind of journey to heaven would always be seen as a higher revelation than an initial call or conversion involving the epiphany of the God.

85. This should be compared with the discussion above on Paul's boasting. He is able to maintain his weakness and his unworthiness, while at the same time leaving no doubt that his labor and accomplishment *through Christ* is beyond anyone else's.

86. The doxology now found at the end of Romans (16:25-27), through perhaps non-Pauline, is interesting to compare with this language in Rom. 1:5; 15:18. There the mission to the Gentiles is spoken of as a "mystery" or secret, an idea that was carried on into deutero-Pauline circles (Col. 1:26-27; Eph. 3:4-6).

87. On these difficult verses see Munck, *Christ and Israel*, pp. 131-38 and his revised treatment in *Paul and the Salvation of Mankind*, pp. 36-55. In the latter he has accepted Cullmann's thesis that Paul refers to himself as the one who "restrains" the coming of the "Man of sin" in 2 Thess. 2:6-7. Although I doubt the Pauline authorship of 2 Thess., the general point still has value. Paul does link the timing of the events of the End with his own work of preaching to the Gentiles.

88. See D. M. Stanley, "The Theme of the Servant of Yahweh in Primitive Christian Soteriology and its Transformation by St. Paul," *CBQ* 16 (1954): 385-425 and Hans Windisch, *Paulus und Christus: Ein biblisch-religionsgeschichtliches Vergleich* (Leipzig: J. C. Hinrichs, 1934), pp. 147-50.

89. In 2 Cor. 9:12 Paul describes this same collection as a "ministry of priestly service (*leitourgias*)." On the collection see Munck, *Paul and the Salvation of Mankind*, pp. 287-97; 301-5; Dieter Georgi, *Die Geschichte der Kollekte des Paulus fur Jerusalem* (Hamburg: Herbert Reich Verlag, 1965); Keith F. Nickle, *The Collection: A study in Paul's Strategy* (Naperville, Ill.: Allenson, 1966). All three agree that this collection had an eschatological meaning for Paul, tied up with his understanding of his mission to the Gentiles and the

subsequent conversion of Israel.

90. This theme also appears in the deutero-Pauline materials. In Col. 1:24 Paul speaks of completing what is "lacking in Christ's sufferings." On this subject see Guttgemanns, *Der liedende Apostel*, pp. 323-28; Dunn, *Jesus and the Spirit*, pp. 326-42.

91. See Blass & Debrunner, *Greek Grammar* pp. 146-47, on this use of the plural.

92. The word appears only here in the N.T. and refers to a play or what one sees at a theater. The imagery is vivid--Paul is on stage with the heavenly and earthly cosmos as the audience. This idea that the heavenly world is interested in and involved with Paul's ministry is carried into the deutero-Pauline materials (see Eph. 3:8-10).

93. These two phrases have similar meanings, referring to that which is "removed by cleansing," and thus, by extension, they can carry the idea of propitiatory offering, ransom, or sacrifice. See Walter Bauer, *A Greek-English Lexicon*, 2d ed., rev. F. Wilbur Gingrich and Frederick W. Danker (Chicago: University of Chicago Press, 1979), pp. 647, 653.

94. Adolf Diessmann (*Bible Studies* [Edinburgh: T & T Clark, 1901], pp. 346-60) understood this curious reference in the light of a magical formula in the Leyden Papyrus. See Betz, *Galatians*, pp. 323-25 for a recent discussion.

95. See Gerhard Sass, *Apostelamt und Kirche: Eine theologisch-exegetische Untersuchung des paulinischen Apostelbegriffs* (Munich: C. Kaiser, 1939), p. 90.

96. See *Mysticism*, pp. 136-37. Schweitzer further speculates that it was Paul's ascent to Paradise that "contributed to the creation of his hope of being rapt away to Jesus." Also see the very important forthcoming article by Arthur Droge, "*MORI LUCRUM*: Paul and Ancient Theories of Suicide," *HTR* 80 (1987). Paul's language shows that he has some kind of "death by choice" in mind. Like John's Jesus, ("no one takes my life ... ") his death will be according to plan.

97. See Davies, *Paul*, pp. 308-19. Lincoln has one of the best standard treatments of the issues involved here, and refers to the important secondary literature; *Paradise Now and Not Yet*, pp. 55-71; 87-109. Lincoln concludes that Paul's language about "being with Christ" refers to the final age "proleptically enjoyed in heaven in the intermediate state," i.e., "now and not yet." Although his solution at least tries to preserve Paul's consistency in the short time between the writing of 1 Thess., 1 and 2 Cor., and Phil., I still think it is more likely he is speaking of his own personal situation.

98. In *Paul and the Salvation of Mankind*, 43.

CHAPTER THREE

THE HEAVENLY JOURNEY IN ANTIQUITY

In this chapter I shall investigate the motif of the heavenly journey in a host of variant texts from the Hellenistic period. My purpose is to ask whether and in what ways such materials shed light upon Paul's report of being caught up to Paradise. The ubiquity of the ascent motif, in texts of the widest range of type and provenance, raises a complex set of questions and problems.

There is the question of the type of journey reported in a given text. Some deal with the ascent of the soul, while others speak of a bodily ascension or assumption into heaven. Still others, as in the case of Paul's account, make no distinction regarding "in the body" or "out of the body," or are unclear about the matter. We read of the ascent of the soul at death, of bodily assumption at the end of life (perhaps in lieu of death), or even of an ascent after death and bodily resurrection (as in the case of Jesus in Luke-Acts). There are accounts of journeys to heaven during the life of a figure, in the sense of a visit or trip, with a return of descent. Sometimes the ascent comes in a dream, or is reported as a vision, or is something visibly seen by observers.

Then there is the problem of the type of text reporting such heavenly journeys. Sometimes the journey is set in the life of a legendary figure, reporting what that individual saw or experienced, or merely asserting that such a one was taken up. In the case of Paul we have the rare example of an identifiable, autobiographical account. There are texts which offer initiation into the secret lore involved in ascent, relating *how* one might achieve an experience. Others report the experience of some contemporary person. Still others merely mention the concept of heavenly ascent, without reporting the experience of anyone. There are even texts which draw upon the motif for purposes of satire or parody.

There is also the question of the consequence and significance of the reported experience. Is the ascent seen as a means of receiving revelation? Is it a transforming or salvific experience? Does it function to confirm a set of beliefs about the heavenly world? Is the experience to be regarded as unique and extraordinary, or as something to be imitated by others? Is the recipient to report the experience or keep it secret?

THINGS UNUTTERABLE: PAUL'S ASCENT TO PARADISE

Such questions, and my account is by no means exhaustive, underlie the very problematic nature of the investigation I propose. Indeed, in view of the problems of categorization, definition, and description, one may ask whether such texts can even be related to one another on the basis of the heavenly journey motif.[1] One must take account of such differences and proceed with caution in attempting to generalize. Nonetheless, I am convinced that ascent to heaven is a *characteristic* expression of Hellenistic piety, and as such is related to a relatively widespread set of shared perceptions. It is this which justifies such generalization.

Dissolution and Rebuilding

Martin Nilsson has characterized the Hellenistic age, seen as the peculiar complex of political, social, cultural, scientific, and religious realities set in motion with the conquests of Alexander the Great, as one of *dissolution and rebuilding*.[2] An old world was passing away and a new one coming to birth. One of the fundamental features of this process, which affected various archaic religions of the period, was the emergence of what he calls a "new cosmology."[3] The archaic cosmology, known to us from Homer, dominant in the Classical period, and reflected in various Ancient Near Eastern texts (including most Hebrew Bible materials), was that of a three-storied universe.[4] The earth was seen as a flat disk surrounded by water (Chaos). Below was the underworld (Hades/Sheol/*kur-nu-gi-a*), the dreary and shadowy abode of the dead. Above was the vault of heaven, the place of the sun, moon, and stars. Still higher was Heaven, dwelling of the gods. There was a celebration of order, as something *won*, a victory over chaos. The regular seasons, the courses of the heavenly bodies, the cycles of life upon earth--as a part of this order--were guaranteed by the gods. The earth was man's place, there he was at home. Death, the origin of which was variously explained, was seen as irreversible and thought to be a gloomy state in which a mere shadow of the former person existed in the underworld, removed from the world of light and life. The gods were *close at hand*, frequently making visits to earth to deal directly with men, or to appear in dreams and visions, or communicate through signs and omens. The human purpose was to serve the gods, to conform to the decreed order of society, to offer prayer and sacrifice. All was in place--the earth was *the place to be*. Jonathan Smith has characterized religions of this period as "religions of etiquette." He comments:

> At the centre of these religions were complex systems governing the interrelationships between gods and men, individuals and the state, living men and their ancestors. The entire cosmos was conceived as a vast network of relationships, each component of which, whether divine or human must *know its place and fulfill its appointed role* .... Through astrology, divination, and oracles man discerned the unalterable patterns of destiny and sought to

bring his world (the microcosm) into harmony with the divine cosmos.[5]

Despite specific variations and exceptions, I find Nilsson's generalizations regarding this archaic cosmology of value, particularly this perception of the earth as the human place. What is important, with regard to the notion of the journey to heaven, are not the differences one finds in various texts which describe and map out the details of such a cosmos, but the rather uniform perception that humans belong on earth, while the realm of the immortal gods is in heaven.[6] I now turn to a number of representative texts which illustrate this general description.

In the Hebrew Bible the celebration of the order and bounds of creation is a common theme.[7] Psa. 74:12-17 illustrates the idea rather sharply:

Yet God my King is from of old,
working salvation in the midst of
the earth.
You divided the sea by your
might;
you broke the heads of the
dragons on the waters.
You crushed the heads of Leviathan,
you gave him as food for
the creatures of the wilderness.
You broke open springs and brooks;
you dried up ever-flowing
streams.
Yours is the day, yours also the night;
you have established the luminaries and the sun.
You have fixed all the bounds of
the earth;
you have made summer and winter.[8]

Although the Psalm begins with the cry, "O God, why do you cast us off forever?" and is a plea for God to act in behalf of the pious, the verses I have quoted form the *basis* of any such expectation. This Psalm not only celebrates God's power, but it affirms the earth as the human place. God has fixed all the bounds so it is here and now that he must act, in the space and order of things which he has established. Psa. 104 also expresses this order of creation, with man at home in the world. God has "set the earth on its foundations, so that it should never be shaken" (v.5). He has won victory over the waters (chaos) and "set a bound which they should not pass" (vv. 6-9). The whole creation is in order, following the established decrees of heaven; and this placing of plants, animals, humans, and the heavenly bodies is *celebrated* with praise and joy (vv. 10-30). Even the cycles of life and death are affirmed as God's decree (vv. 29-30). Related to this view of human place is the idea of death as a journey down to Sheol.[9] Psa. 88 is the prayer of a dying man who pleads for extended life:

> For my soul is full of troubles
> and my life draws near to Sheol.
> I am reckoned among those who go
> down to the Pit;
> I am a man who has no strength,
> like one forsaken among the dead,
> like the slain that lie in the grave,
> like those whom you
> remember no more,
> for they are cut off from your hand (vv. 3-5).

Sheol is a journey *down*, it is undesired, and most important, it is a place or state where one is forsaken and cut off from God, where one is remembered no more. In the following verses the author asks a series of rhetorical questions:

> Do you work wonders for the
> dead?
> Do the shades rise up to praise
> you?
> Is your steadfast love declared in the
> grave?
> or your faithfulness in Abbaddon?
> Are your wonders known in the
> darkness,or your saving help in the land of forgetfulness?
> (vv. 10-12)

Such an understanding of death and Sheol is found throughout the Hebrew Bible and continues well into the Second Temple period.[10] Psa. 115:16-18 offers an epitome of the cosmological structure of the Hebrew Bible, and except for the particular reference to Yahweh, could well represent the archaic period in general:

> The heavens are Yahweh's heavens,
> but *the earth he has given to the
> sons of men.*
> The dead do not praise Yahweh,
> nor do any that go down into
> silence.
> But we will bless Yahweh
> from this time forth and for
> evermore.

Such a three-tiered cosmology, with its sense of boundary and place, whether always celebrated or not, is nonetheless accepted as the decreed order of things.

The Sumerian poem, "The Creation of the Pickax," further illustrates the main features of this archaic cosmology. This text, from the third millennium B.C.E., well expresses the affirmation and celebration of order so characteristic of this period:

> The lord, he who truly created *the normal order*,
> The lord, whose decisions are inalterable,
> Enlil, who brings up the seed of the land from
> the earth,
> Took care to move away heaven and earth,
> Took care to move away earth from heaven,
> Did truly speed to remove heaven from earth,
> So that the seed from which grew the nation
> could sprout up from the field.
> He bound up the gash in the bond between
> heaven and earth,
> *So that mankind could grow* from the earth.

The poem continues, relating the creation of the workman's pickax:

> He brought the pickax into existence as the
> day came forth,
> He introduced labor and *decreed fate*,
> the pickman's *way of life*.

The poem concludes with praise to the god, with a celebration of the order of creation and the decree of fate as represented by the pickax:

> The pickax, its fate decreed by father Enlil,
> The pickax is exalted![11]

This order, established from the beginning, provides human kind its proper place. There is the sense of creating or making space for man. Within that allotted place are decreed a whole set of fates or ways of life, here illustrated by the lowly pickman. Man's duty to the gods involves an affirmation of that place: of his place in the cosmos and his role within the society of men.[12]

The ancient Mesopotamian view of death and afterlife is strikingly similar to Hebrew concepts of Sheol. In the well known *Gilgamesh Epic*, the hero Gilgamesh, during his hazardous journey to find Uta-napishtim (a kind of Babylonian Noah), and learn the secrets of immortality, is admonished by Sidiru:

> Gilgamesh, whither rovest thou?
> The life thou pursuest thou shall not find.

> When the gods created mankind,
> *Death for mankind they set aside,*
> *Life in their own hand retaining.*
> Thou, Gilgamesh, let full be thy belly,
> Make thou merry by day and by night.
> Of each day make thou a feast of rejoicing,
> Day and night dance thou and play![13]

Enkidu, the hero's friend, had already described to Gilgamesh the world of the dead. Before he died he had dreamed of descending to *kur-nu-gi-a*, the "land of no return." He was taken to the "House of Darkness":

> To the house which none leave
> who have entered it,
> On the road from which there
> is no way back,
> To the house wherein the dwellers
> are bereft of light,
> Where dust is their fare
> and clay their food.[14]

In this "house of dust" all the dead are stripped of earthly rank and status and share a common gloom or misery.

A somewhat similar three-tiered cosmology is found in later Greek materials. Hesiod's *Theogony* offers a representative description:[15]

> Truly at the first Chaos came to be,
> but then wide-bosomed Earth, the ever-sure
> foundation of all,
> and dim Tartarus in the depth of wide-pathed
> earth . . .,
> And earth first bore equal to herself,
> Starry heaven, to cover her on every side,
> to be an ever-sure place for the blessed gods.[16]

After a series of troubles Zeus banishes the Titans, guaranteeing to man that the present order will last forever (lines 713-35). The Homeric hymn, "To Earth the Mother of All," well expresses this sense of celebration of the earth as the human place.

> I will sing of well-founded Earth, mother of all,
> eldest of all beings.
> She feeds all creatures that are in the world,
> all that go upon the goodly land,
> and all that are in the paths of the sea,

> and all that fly:
> all these are fed of her store.
> Through you, O queen, men are blessed in
> their children
> and blessed in their harvests,
> and to you it belongs to give means
> of life to mortal men
> and to take it away.[17]

The archaic view of the Greek Hadean world is strikingly similar to Hebrew and Mesopotamian concepts. In the Homeric epics a shadowy replica of the living person (*eidōlon*) descends into Hades at death, living on in dismal gloom. This is best illustrated by Achilles' famous reply to Odysseus when the latter makes his journey to Hades and encounters the shade of the dead hero, seeking to reconcile him to his fate:

> Nay, seek not to speak soothingly to me of death, glorious Odysseus. I should choose, so I might live on earth, to serve as the hireling of another, of some portionless man whose livelihood was but small, rather than to be lord over all the dead who have perished.[18]

Nilsson asserts that during the Hellenistic period one can begin to speak of a "new cosmology," which was related to a fundamental shift in man's perception of his place.[19] In this cosmology the earth is the center and lowest level of a vast and expanded universe. It is surrounded by planetary spheres or "heavens," usually seven in number, each dominated by its respective powers.[20] Below the moon, the first of these spheres, is the "air," the abode of various spirits or *daimones*. Above the highest sphere is the pure dwelling of God. Human beings are separated from God, therefore, by an interminable distance, filled with intermediate powers. Dwelling at the lowest level of this vast cosmos, they are no longer at home. They are out of place. Their destiny is to dwell with God in the highest heaven, free from the bonds of death and the mortality of the body. The language of exile is common--men are strangers and pilgrims in this sensible world. Salvation comes to mean "getting out" or going home, i.e., to be released from the earthly condition and obtain immortality in heaven. Most religions of the period were concerned with explaining how man has become what he is, calling him to turn from his present condition and preparing him for his release so he can realize his lofty heavenly destiny. Of course there are important differences among various systems. Some have a notion of a Savior figure, who opens the way, while others do not. There is a range of attitudes toward the cosmos, from worshipful adoration to rebellion. The explanations of how humans have fallen into mortal conditions vary, as do the corresponding solutions or ways of "salvation". Still, there seems to be a fairly widespread perception within most of these religions that man is out of place and that he can escape the lower world and achieve immortality. Jonathan Smith has defined the study of Hellenistic religions as "the study of archaic Mediterranean religions in their Hellenistic *phase* within their native and diasporic setting."[21] He isolates a number of characteristic "shifts" as archaic religions move into this new context. Religions are concerned more with salvation of the individual in contrast to that of the nation. There is a corresponding shift from "birthright" (national) to "convinced" religions (i.e., religions of conversion). Rather than a celebration of the order of the cosmos, one often encounters a sense of alienation from the created world. The figure of the "holy man" or magician replaces the notion of the sacred temple as a locus for contact with the deity. Of course none of these shifts are absolute. One encounters, to use Smith's language again, "the dynamics of persistence and change."[22] Therefore, we are not dealing with strictly chronological designations in speaking of the "archaic" and the "Hellenistic." Throughout the period one finds texts in which the archaic notions survive, but they are are combined with or adapted to these characteristically dualistic perceptions of human beings and their universe.[23] Smith characterizes religions of the period as follows:

> The religious man sought to make contact with, or to stand before, this one, true god of the Beyond. The piety of the individual was directed either toward preparing himself to ascend up through the planetary spheres to the realm of the transcendent god or toward calling the transcendent god down that he might appear to him in an epiphany or vision. These techniques for achieving ascent or epiphany make up the bulk of material that has usually been termed magical, theurgic . . . or astrological and that represents the characteristic expression of Hellenistic religiosity.[24]

The "Dream of Scipio" in Cicero's *Republic* provides a representative illustration of this new cosmology.[25] Cicero recounts the dream of Scipio Africanus, in which his grandfather, Africanus the Elder (of Carthage fame), now deceased, appears to him. Scipio is lifted high above the earth and Africanus the Elder reveals the workings of the cosmos to him. Scipio wants to know first whether those "whom we think of as dead [including his father Paulus] were really still alive." He is told:

> Surely all those are alive . . . who have escaped the bondage of the body as from a prison; but that *life* of yours, which men so call, *is really death* (6. 14).

Scipio wants to immediately die, so he can hasten to the heavenly world; whereupon Africanus the Elder explains that all must remain on earth until called home by God. The duty of men on earth must first be fulfilled, described in this text, chiefly, as loyalty to family and country and the development of virtues. Africanus declares:

> Such a life is the road to the skies, to that gathering of those who have completed their earthly lives and have been relieved of the body and who live in yonder place which you see now (6.16).

Scipio is carried away with the beauty of the heavenly world, which he now beholds at close range. Looking down at the tiny earth, he is scornful of its comparative insignificance. Africanus then describes this heavenly cosmos:

> How long will your thoughts be fixed upon the lowly earth? Do you not see what lofty circles, or rather spheres, by which the whole is joined. One of them, the outermost, is that of heaven; it contains all the rest, and is itself the supreme God, holding and embracing within itself all the other spheres; in it are fixed the eternal revolving courses of the stars. Beneath it are seven other spheres which revolve in the opposite direction to that of heaven. One of these globes is that light which on earth is called Saturn's . . . Jupiter . . . Mars . . . Sun . . . Venus and Mercury . . . and in the lowest sphere revolves the Moon . . . . But below the Moon there is nothing except what is mortal and doomed to decay, save only the souls given to the human race by the bounty of the gods, while above the Moon all things are eternal. For the ninth and central sphere, which is the earth, is immovable and the lowest of all, and toward it all ponderable bodies are drawn by their own natural tendency downward (6.17).

Africanus reveals to his pupil further secrets of the cosmos, exhorting him, "Keep your gaze fixed upon these heavenly things, and scorn the earthly" (6. 19). Such a contemplation of the eternal heavenly world will lead to a "true reward, a return" to the heavenly regions (6. 23).[26] The dialogue continues with Africanus' classic statement on dualism:

> Strive on indeed, and be sure that it is not you that is mortal, but only your body. For that man whom your outward form reveals is not yourself; the spirit is the true self, not that physical figure which can be pointed out by the finger. Know then, that you are a god, if a god is that which lives, feels, remembers, and foresees, and which rules, governs, and moves the body over which it is set, just as the supreme God above rules this universe. (6. 24).

This cosmology, with its perception of man's place, is fairly standard. There is an emphasis on the individual, who at death will leave the mortal body behind, ascending back to heaven, the true home of the soul. A devaluation of all that is earthly and material runs through the entire text. Since humans don't belong on earth, death is viewed positively, as a release to "true life." The text lacks any myth of the soul's fall into the lower world and its imprisonment in the body. The planetary spheres exert influence below, but neither their powers, nor details of the soul's ascent, are described with any detail. The general attitude toward the cosmos is positive. One is to contemplate the heavenly world with all its harmony, thus disassociating oneself from the material world below.

Poimandres, the first tractate of the *Corpus Hermeticum*, contains a similar cosmological structure, but illustrates some of the variations that are found in this kind of material.[27] The author (disciple) opens the work with an account of a visionary experience in which he sees an immense figure who reveals himself as "Poimandres, the Mind of Absolute Power," The text then recounts a revelation of the origin of mankind, how he came to be subject to fate and death, the present state of man as he is, and the way he can return to the heavens. The account of human origins and the fall reflects a complicated cosmogony (12-19). As in the "Dream of Scipio," there are seven planetary spheres which, in this text, administer Fate (9, 25). In his fallen condition man is mortal, but Poimandres declares:

> And because of this, man alone, of all the living creatures upon earth, is twofold. He is mortal because of his body, but immortal because of his essential being. For even though he is immortal and has authority over everything, he suffers mortal conditions, being subject to Fate; although therefore he is above the order of the spheres, he has become a slave to it . . . and is held fast. (15).[28]

One is saved through the power of God, who comes to rescue (*boetheia*) those who recognize the truth about their natures, turn from attachments to the material world, and prepare for the ascent back to heaven (22). This ascent is described in 24-26. As one rises through the planetary spheres, he is released from all the powers which enslaved him, finally joining God. His final destiny is apotheosis (*theothēnai*)--recovering all that was lost in his fall and regaining immortal heavenly existence. The cosmological structure is similar to that of "Scipio's Dream," but in a radicalized form. The seven planetary spheres are viewed negatively, as separating man from God. Human life on earth is not merely of less value than immortal heavenly life, it is a mistake, the result of deception and lust. Still, fundamentally, it is similar to Cicero's account: the devaluation of the earthly, death viewed as a positive release, an emphasis on heaven as the proper human place--all characteristic perceptions within this new cosmology. Other texts would yield further variations in detail, but these fundamentals are often present in this kind of material.[29]

2 Enoch provides a good example of a Jewish text which reflects this Hellenistic cosmology. Enoch is taken up through seven levels of heaven, learning the various cosmic secrets associated with each. He finally arrives at the seventh heaven where he is taken before God's throne and glorified. We have other examples of Jewish-Christian and Christian texts, such as the

Ascension of Isaiah, which reflect a similar cosmological structure.[30] Jean Daniélou offers the following summary comment on the Christian material:

> It has been necessary to dwell on this question of the structure of the celestial world because it was to play an important part in Jewish Christian dogmatic teaching. Indeed, the principal dogmas were formulated in terms of cosmology. The incarnation was presented as a descent of the Word through the angelic spheres; the Passion as Christ's combat with the angels of the air, followed by the descent into Hell; the Resurrection as an exaltation of Christ's humanity above all the angelic spheres; and on its way encountering their guardians, to whom it would have to render account. All these conceptions are based on a vision of the heavenly spheres which is part of the framework of Jewish Christianity.[31]

I would only change the last sentence to read "which is a part of the framework of most religions of the period." The point is Jews and Christians worked out the various forms of their religious systems within the same general cosmological framework. Often Jewish and Christian materials dealing with the idea of ascent have been handled under the rubric of "apocalypticism," but the phenomenon of apocalypticism itself typically reflects the religious development of the Hellenistic period, especially with regard to cosmological structure. Whether Robert Grant was right or wrong about "gnosticism" developing *out of* a Jewish apocalyptic milieu, he, along with Daniélou and others have clearly shown the common "background" (or really, "foreground") these materials share and develop.[32] Hans Dieter Betz aptly points out:

> The underlying questions which have led to the development of dualism, angelology, cosmology, astrology and so forth, are to a large extent identical with the basic problems which occupy the entire period of Hellenism, and which have precipitated parallel doctrines there. We have to free ourselves from the idea of treating apocalypticism as an isolated and purely inner-Jewish phenomenon. Rather, we must learn to understand apocalypticism as a peculiar manifestation within the entire course of Hellenistic oriental syncretism.[33]

Betz' comment is supported by the work of many scholars (E. R. Goodenough, A. D. Nock, Robert Grant, Saul Liebermann, Morton Smith, Jacob Neusner, Jonathan Smith, to name a few). The broad compartmentalization of "Judaism" from "Hellenism" is invalid. All religions of this period, including forms of Judaism, *are* Hellenistic religions, and must be seen in that broader context. In this regard, even various forms of "gnosticism" represent a radicalized structural possibility within this same general history, rather than genuinely "new" religions. Plato is not so far from *Poimandres,* despite the protests of Plotinus--if one takes into account the broader perspective which this transition from archaic to Hellenistic provides.[34] Similarly, Paul's scheme of salvation (even with his "Jewish" idea of resurrection and apocalyptic view of the end of history), set in this broader context, shares much with a "gnostic" text such as *Poimandres*.[35]

In the light of this new cosmology, I would stress two basic points about the heavenly journey. First, whenever there is the belief that mortal man can ascend to immortal life in heaven, we are not dealing with the mere notion of possibility, rather, more often than not, there is the idea that heaven is, in fact, *his place*. E. R. Dodds called this "the progressive devaluation" of life in the material world.[36] It is a prime characteristic of Hellenistic religiosity. Still, I would qualify this somewhat. When I speak of humans "belonging" in heaven--this whole notion of "human place"-- I intend it to be taken as a matter of degrees. There are Hellenistic systems which clearly see human beings as *misplaced* on earth, trapped in mortal bodies (e.g., forms of gnosticism). While others would see it more as a matter of stages or development. Mortal, earthly life is not so much a mistake as a first stage (like caterpillars and butterflies) to a higher transformed life. I am using "belong" in this qualified way, meaning final and proper place. There are degrees to this depending on the religious system. Where Paul belongs in this regard is debatable. On the one hand, given all his language about transformation and the new body, he might be seen as a prime example of this latter type. The creation is good, but presently limited. Immortality is a stage beyond the mortal. But as a Jew he accepts some version of the Eden story, which tells of the entrance of death into the world. So presumably death or mortality is some kind of failure or mistake. At one point he says that *God* introduced this state he calls "bondage to decay," with some sort of plan in mind (Rom. 8:20). But he also attributes death to sin, and seems to connect it to Satanic forces in the cosmos (Rom. 5:12; 1 Cor. 15:20-28). So Paul's view of the matter is not entirely clear. Still, he does think that full and proper human potential involves immortal heavenly life, and that is my main point here. The second point I would stress is that during this period, movement between the realms of heaven and earth, whether by gods or men, is increasingly seen as a difficult or even dangerous enterprise.[37] In spatial terms one can speak of distance--a greatly expanded universe--but what is often involved is the belief that a host of intermediate (usually hostile) powers separate humans from the higher levels of heaven. It is just this perception which accounts for most of the movement between the divine and earthly realms, gods coming down to deal intimately with mortal men, mortals going up to receive revelations or immortality. In either case power is needed over the forces which separate the two realms. This point also needs some qualification. For example, in Cicero's tale of Scipio's dream, the ascent of the soul to the astral zones sounds relatively danger free, almost automatic (although at the end he does include, following Plato's model, some nasty things about what can happen to those who do not qualify for this "road to the stars"). I think this might have to do with the type of text one is considering. Cicero is offering us an armchair adventure, a tale modeled on Plato's myth of Er at the end of the *Republic*. It does give him a way to push some of his republican political virtues, but that is about it. It is useful as a typical reflection of popular cosmology and dualism. But people *did* take this matter of ascent very seriously. There are texts telling "how to do it" in the Greek magical papyri, and Paul, our single autogiographical example from the period, comes back with his "thorn in the flesh." It could be that the "danger level" has to do with the degree the text reflects some actual practice or experience of ascent, or with just how seriously the text deals with the subject. *Poimandres* is a very serious text, and really serves as a kind of "Genesis" revelation, telling how things became as they are and how to escape. So, given these qualifications, I would consider these factors basic to an evaluation of ascent in this period.

Types of Heavenly Ascent

Despite the variations I have pointed out in ascent materials, I want to attempt a system of classification. I have one limited operating question or concern, since in the end I want to shed some light on Paul's ascent text. What is the purpose or outcome of the heavenly journey in the text which reports it? I am proposing four basic types of ascent in this regard: (1) Ascent as an invasion of heaven (2) Ascent to receive revelation; (3) Ascent to heavenly immortality; (4) Ascent as a foretaste of the heavenly world. One can point out texts in which there is a good deal of mixing and merging, so I would stress that these are working models rather than absolute types. Generally speaking, my first two categories are more characteristic of the "archaic" period, while the second two are more typically "Hellenistic."

1. Ascent as an Invasion of Heaven

In my sketch of the archaic cosmology I emphasized the elements of celebration and affirmation of the order and bounds of creation, with man's place therein as an earth-bound mortal. This has direct bearing on the motif of the heavenly journey. Within such a cosmic structure we do find accounts of journeys to heaven, however, these are essentially accounts of invasion, of humans breaking the bounds; of man out of place. Indeed, such stories are often told to make this very point--that one is *not* to ascend to heaven.

In an Akkadian text, Adapa, the son of Ea, through his powerful curse breaks "the wing of the south wind," incurring the wrath of Anu, king of the gods.[38] Ea tells him that he is to go up to heaven to appear before Anu, to work out a scheme by which Anu's wrath can be appeased. Ea knows that Anu will offer Adapa the food of the gods, which confers immortality. He tells his son that it is, in fact, the "food of death," and he is therefore to refuse it. The ascent account begins:

He made him take the road to heaven,
and to heaven he went up (lines 37-38).

All transpires as Ea planned; Adapa is offered the food but refuses it and Anu declares: "Thou shall not have (eternal) life! Ah per[ver]se mankind!" and Adapa is cast back down to earth. The basic myth is now embedded in an incantation. It is difficult to interpret, but seems to be an explanation of why mankind is not immortal.[39] Ascent here is viewed negatively, as an invasion of heaven, reinforcing the view that the earth is the human place, that mortality is man's lot.

A somewhat different story is told of Etana, listed as one of the legendary rulers of the Sumerian dynasty of Kish. He is described as "Etana, a shepherd, the one who to heaven ascended."[40] The texts which tell of his ascent are fragmentary. He must go to heaven and bring down the "plant of birth" so that he can reproduce. By enlisting the aid of an eagle he is taken up. At this point the text breaks off, so we cannot determine the results of his journey. In one version of the Neo-Assyrian recension he falls back to the earth.[41] After rising up a league the eagle says, "My friend, cast a glance at how the land [appears]! . . . . And the wide sea is just like a tub." Then at the second league he says, "My friend, cast a glance at how the land appears! The land has turned into a furrow [. . .], and the wide sea is just like a bread basket." When he reaches the third league he apparently becomes fearful, declaring, "My friend, I will not ascend to heaven!" He begins to fall, and the text breaks off at this point. It may be that in some versions of the tale he is successful in obtaining the plant, since the king list records the name of his son. But in this text at least, the author presents the story as a parody of a human out of his element.

The *Assyrian Dream-Book* contains several fascinating sections which interpret the meaning of a dream in which one ascends to heaven. Column IV of the Susa tablet reads in part:

> If a man [in his dream] ascends [to heaven] and the
> go[ds bless him: this man] will die.
> If a man [in his dream] ascends [to heaven] and the
> gods [curse him: this man will live long].[42]

Such a text, with its lack of context, is difficult to interpret, but I would read it as a negative appraisal of ascent which makes use of the language of reversal: to be blessed going up is actually to die; to be cursed going up is to live. The point is, that even in a dream, humans must not travel to heaven.

In the Hebrew Bible one finds a similarly negative appraisal of ascent. The ironic language of Prov. 30:2-4 (recalling Job 26; 38:1-42:6), though not a tale of ascent, emphasizes the contrast between the human and divine realms:

> Who has ascended to heaven and
> come down?
> Who has gathered the wind in his
> fists?
> Who has wrapped up the waters in
> his garments?
> Who has established all the ends
> of the earth?
> What is his name, and what is his
> son's name?
> Surely you know! (v. 4, RSV)

A somewhat similar idea lies behind Deut. 29:29 and 30:11-14. There is no need for one to ascend to heaven to learn the "secret things" which belong to God. Rather, man's task is to perform the commandments of Torah which relate to his life upon earth.[43] Such an emphasis runs throughout much of the Hebrew Bible. The idea is pointedly expressed in Sirach 3:21-22:

> Seek not what is too difficult for
> you,
> nor investigate what is beyond
> your power.
> Reflect upon what has been
> assigned to you,
> for you do not need what is
> hidden.[44]

A direct protest against ascent is found in Isa. 14:12-20. In its present form it is a taunt against the king of Babylon who says in his heart, "I will ascend to heaven; above the stars of God . . ., I will make myself like the Most High" (vv. 13-14, RSV). Instead he falls down to the depths of Sheol, the place of worms and maggots (v. 11). The contrast between the heights of heaven and the lower regions of Sheol is absolute, the fall is a total one. The myth of the fall of a divine being (the "Morning Star" v. 12) may lie behind this text, but here it is about a man (v. 16), and ascent is an invasion stemming from the pride of one who seeks to go beyond human bounds and become like a god.[45]

In Greek materials, I am aware of no specific tale of ascent from the archaic period which would parallel these examples from the Ancient Near East. In Greek tradition the gods live in the mountains, or at the ends of the earth (like Helios and Selena), and of course there is no cult of the stars at this period. This likely accounts for our lack of texts. There is, however, Lucian's *Icaromenippus*, from the Roman imperial period, which typifies the idea of ascent to heaven as invasion.[46] Lucian presents his entertaining and satirical story within the framework of a conversation between Menippus, his main character, and a friend. Menippus claims to have just returned from a visit to heaven, to the very citadel of Zeus. Although he speaks of a three-stage flight--from moon, to sun, to heaven--the distance is not so great.

THINGS UNUTTERABLE: PAUL'S ASCENT TO PARADISE

Menippus makes the journey using the wings of an eagle and a vulture. There is no difficulty in ascending, no move through any threatening planetary spheres. The ascent is bodily and lacks any idea of movement from a material into a spiritual realm. It is obvious that Lucian has cast his story in an archaic cosmological framework. Still, the journey is regarded as extraordinary. Menippus reports to his friends:

> Here I am, I tell you, just come back today from the very presence of your great Zeus himself, and *I have seen and heard wonderful things.* If you don't believe me, I am overjoyed, precisely because my good fortune is beyond belief (2).[47]

His desire to make the flight stemmed from despair over ever learning the truth about the cosmos. He had tired of the vain and contradictory theories of the philosophers:

> At my wits end in view of all this, I despaired of hearing any truth about these matters on earth and thought that the only way out of my whole dilemma would be to get wings and somehow go up to heaven (10).

The account of his arrival at the gate of heaven and his reception illustrates this archaic idea of ascent as invasion:

> At first I made up my mind to go straight in without much more ado, for I thought I should easily *escape observation*, as I was half eagle and I knew that the eagle was on intimate terms with Zeus from of old; but afterwards I concluded that they would very soon *find me out* because the other wing that I wore was a vulture's. Thinking it best, anyhow, not to take any unnecessary changes, I went up and knocked at the door. Hermes answered my knock, *inquired my name*, and went off in haste to tell Zeus. In a little while *I was admitted in great fear and trembling*, and found them all sitting together, not without apprehension themselves, for *my visit, being so unprecedented*, had put them in quite a flutter, and they almost expected the whole human race to arrive at any moment, provided with wings like mine (22).

Although he is finally welcomed by Zeus, he is told that his visit is to be only for a day or two, then he will be "sent away" (23). While on his visit, Menippus observes some of the activities of the gods and listens to a speech in which Zeus exposes the Stoics, Academics, Epicureans and Peripatetics for the foolishness of their philosophies (29-32). He then announces that Menippus must be stripped of his wings, "*that he may never come again*"; whereupon he is carried back to earth by the god Hermes (34).

This tale could also be placed in my next category, ascent to receive a revelation, since Menippus claims to have "seen and heard wonderful things" and learns, from the divine point of view, the vanity of all human philosophies. Strictly speaking, if I stay with my stated question, i.e., the function of the story in its context, it does belong there. Although it is a parody, Lucian uses the motif to criticize the philosophies of men by means of revelation received on a heavenly journey. This illustrates my point about overlapping categories. I have included it here only because it illustrates the archaic framework as well. Menippus is clearly out of place when he flies to heaven, he is seen as a threat to the divine order of things, and his visit is presented as an intrusion, as something exceptional, that must not be repeated.

I present this model as a characteristic, though not exclusive, way of perceiving the journey to heaven in the archaic period. I want to avoid excessive generalization. Even in Homer, as Burkert has pointed out, "the idea of the musty 'House of Hades', hateful to the gods, coexists with that of Elysium and with the apotheosis of Herakles."[48] In the Hebrew Bible there are the well-known tales of Enoch and Elijah (Gen. 5:24; 2 Kings 2:1-12). The notion of a journey "Beyond," to the Isles of the Blessed or some outer region of the earth (as with Gilgamesh's Utnapishtim or Menelaus in Homer), is essentially still a journey out of this world, and is at least related to the idea of ascent to heaven or apotheosis. Still, given the *dominant* perception of man as an earth-bound mortal, the very notion of ascent in this period is fundamentally an intrusion into the divine realm, a tale of man out of place. This, of course, is in the sharpest contrast to the later widespread view that man *belongs* in the heavenly world.

2. Ascent to Receive Revelation

Like my first category, this type of ascent involves a "round trip" from earth to heaven and back again (ascent/descent). In contrast to the previous type, I have in mind examples where the journey is appraised positively. Although the idea of receiving revelation could be present in any of my other three types, I have made this a separate division to focus on texts in which this idea appears to be the main purpose of the journey. I am limiting myself to texts which still see the earth, not heaven, as the human place, so that the ascent remains a "visit," though not an intrusion, into the divine realm. The one going up is favored and selected, but as a mortal must return to the earth where he belongs.

Certain Ancient Near Eastern ideas of royal enthronement seem related to this type of ascent. There is an Enmenduranki, mentioned in a ritual tablet from the library of Assurbanipal, who is called up to heaven:[49]

> Enmeduranki, the k[ing of Sippar],
> the beloved of Anu, Enlil and Ea,

> Shamash into Ebarra [caused him to enter],
> Shamash and Adad to their assembly [called
> him] . . .,
> Shamash and Adad on a great golden throne [placed him],
> to inspect oil on water, the secret of Anu,
> [Enlil and Ea they taught him].
> The tablets of the gods, the bag with the mystery
> of heaven [and earth],
> the cedar staff, the darling of the great gods,
> they caus[ed his hand to seize].[50]

Enmeduranki is the ancestor of the *bārū*-college of priests. The myth serves to confirm the heavenly authority of the mysteries revealed to them. Geo Widengren has traced this motif of royal or prophetic enthronement (ascent, initiation into heavenly secrets, receiving a commission) into later Jewish traditions involving kingship, prophetic commissions and the revelation of secret heavenly lore.[51] The complex literary traditions surrounding Moses' ascent on Mount Sinai (now found in Exodus 24), though not explicitly referring to a journey to heaven, appear related to this pattern which Widengren has isolated.[52] Moses (or alternatively Moses, Aaron, Nadab, Abihu and the seventy elders--24:9-11), in ascending the mountain, enters the presence of God, the realm of the divine. He is given revelation in the form of heavenly tablets, then descends back to the mortal realm. There is no reference in these texts to enthronement or deification.[53] Moses *visits*, but does not belong in, the divine realm. His ascent is a means of receiving revelation, and functions as a *way of claiming heavenly authority* for the laws he is given. Isaiah's prophetic call is another example of this same pattern (Isa. 6:1-13). Since there is no specific reference to him being taken up, this could be termed a "visionary ascent". He sees "Yahweh sitting on a throne, high and lifted up . . . ." (v. 1).[54] In his vision he finds himself before the heavenly court and is given a message and a corresponding prophetic commission. He is then to return to earth to carry it out. As a mortal, he is *out of place* in the divine realm; he cries out "Woe is me! For I am lost; for I am a man of unclean lips, and I dwell in the midst of a people of unclean lips; for my eyes have seen the King, Yahweh of hosts!" He must descend to carry out his mission, but the vision functions to lend heavenly authority to his message. The throne visions of Ezekiel should be compared here (Ezk. 1, 10). Although these chapters lack the explicit motif of ascent to heaven (given the curious notion of a kind of portable throne-chariot in which God rides), even if they are classed as epiphanies, this basic pattern of being called before the divine throne, being given a revelation, and subsequently returning to the realm of mortals is still related. Daniel's vision of the throne of God and the revelations he is given should also be mentioned here (Dan. 7:9-28). The text does not talk about him being taken to heaven and actually appearing before the throne of God, as with Isaiah, but there are similarities between "seeing the throne" and being taken up, particularly the attempt to provide divine sanction for the revealed message.

In later Jewish traditions we find this model of ascent in the complex body of materials now known as *1 (Ethiopic) Enoch*.[55] One of the oldest sections of this collection, the *Book of the Watchers* (chaps. 1-36), tells how the legendary figure Enoch was taken on a heavenly journey and shown the secrets of the cosmos.[56] He sees a number of visions in which various eschatological mysteries are revealed to him, including the fate of the "Watchers"--those fallen angels who had lost their heavenly state (1:1-14:8). He then relates how he was borne up into heaven, appearing before the very presence of God's lofty throne. Here the reference to ascent is explicit. The text dramatically describes the scene:

> And I observed and saw inside it [the house or palace of God] a lofty throne--its appearance was like crystal and its wheels like the shining sun; and (I heard?) the voice of the cherubim; and from beneath the throne were issuing streams of flaming fire. It was difficult to look at it. And the Great Glory was sitting upon it--as for his gown, which was shining more brightly than the sun, it was whiter than any snow. None of the angels was able to come in and see the face of the Excellent and the Glorious One; *and no one of the flesh can see him*--the flaming fire was round about him, and a great fire stood before him. No one could come near unto him from among those that surrounded the tens of millions (that stood) before him. . . . Until then I was prostrate on my face covered and trembling. And the Lord called me with his own mouth and said to me, "Come near to me Enoch, and to my holy Word." And he lifted me up and brought me near to the gate, but I continued to look down with my face (14:18-25).

Enoch is then taken on two tours of the cosmos. First he is shown the underworld, the secrets of meteorology, and told the names and tasks of the various archangels (17-20). Then he is shown more cosmological geography, including Sheol with its punishments, the garden of the righteous with the Tree of Life, and other astronomical mysteries (21-36). The extraordinary nature of Enoch's experience is clearly expressed in this text. Although out of place, he is still allowed this temporary and intimate audience with God, something even denied to angels. The motif of ascent functions as a vehicle of revelation, offering divine authority to the cosmological and eschatological lore in which the circles that composed and preserved this literature must have had an interest.[57] The Greek version of the *Testament of Levi* (2nd. century B.C.E.) draws upon the idea of ascent in a similar way.[58] Levi falls into a deep sleep and an angel of God takes him through the first levels of the heavens (in some manuscripts three, in others seven), revealing the astronomical and eschatological secrets associated with each (2:7-3:3). He is then told that he is to ascend to the highest heaven, brilliant and incomparable, where he will stand before the Lord himself (2:10). There he is given the priesthood and shown the future plans of God (4:1-5:3), whereupon he is brought back down to earth. As in the *Book of the Watchers*, ascent functions as a means of revelation in this text, serving to validate the Levitical priesthood and offering assurance that the Lord will come to judge the world in the last days. The Latin *Life of Adam and Eve* (1st. century C.E) provides still another example.[59] In this text Adam relates his experience to his son Seth:

> Listen, Seth my son, and I will pass on to you what I heard and saw. After your mother and I had been driven out of Paradise, while we were praying, Michael the archangel and messenger of God came to me. And I saw a chariot like the wind and its wheels were fiery. I was carried off into the Paradise of righteousness, and I saw the LORD sitting and his appearance was unbearable flaming fire. And many thousands of angels were at the right and at the left of the chariot (25:1-3).[60]

Before God's throne Adam pleads for mercy and God promises him that the right to serve him will not be removed from his descendants. Michael then seizes him, casting him out of Paradise. At this point some manuscripts contain an apocalyptic piece (possibly a later interpolation) in which Adam relates to Seth all that was revealed to him. Namely, all that will come to pass in the future, including the fortunes of the people of Israel into the time of the Second Temple (29:4-15). This text has some similarities with my first type, that of intrusion, since Adam is *seized and cast out of heaven* (probably echoing the garden of Eden story). But his appearance before the throne of God, however brief, is permitted by God and he does receive revelation. As a final example from Jewish sources around this period there is the *Apocalypse of Abraham* (1st. to 2nd. century C.E.).[61] In chapters 9-32, Abraham, conducted by the angel Iaoel, is borne up above the seventh heaven.[62] He is taken before the chariot throne of God where he is able to look down over all the levels below. God then reveals to him the history of the fall of man, why sin is allowed, how judgment and the final restoration of Israel will be accomplished (21-30). The text envisions a Messianic age with a restored Israel and a rebuilt temple. He returns to earth, assured that his descendants will be vindicated. Abraham's journey obviously provides the means of setting forth the apocalyptic expectations of the author. As with the other examples, it is a way of claiming authoritative revelation directly from God.

In turning to Greek materials I am aware of no text which precisely parallels this pattern, i.e., a mortal taken to heaven, appearing before the throne of the deity, and receiving a commission or revelation. Perhaps the closest is Parmenides' *prooemium*, which survives in a few fragments.[63] He tells of being taken in a chariot through the gate leading from daylight, where he is received and addressed by a goddess:

> Then the goddess welcomed me kindly, took in her hand my right hand, and addressed me, speaking thus, "Young man, who in company with immortal chariot drivers come to our house

> with the horses that carry you, hail! for no bad destiny is it that sent you out to come this way--it is indeed a *way remote from the paths of men*--but that which is right and just. *You are to learn everything*; both the immovable heart of well-rounded truth, and the opinions of mortal men, in which there is no truly convincing force--still, that too you shall learn, how these opinions are to cover everything in acceptable fashion."[64]

In the central section of the poem she expounds to Parmenides the three conceivable methods or "paths of inquiry" in philosophy, one of which she calls the "path of true persuasion."[65] Various interpretations of this journey have been proposed. Some see it as a shamanistic phenomena, while others view it as mere allegory with the journey representing the path of philosophical investigation. It is not entirely clear whether this is a journey to heaven, or a trip to the lower world.[66] What I would note here is the bare pattern, the journey of a mortal to encounter the deity and the reception of revealed truth.

On the whole, for Greeks in the archaic period, revelations come through epiphanies, oracles, dreams, omens, and signs of various sorts--all very "earthly" in their own way--not by appearing before the throne of Zeus. The many examples of the journey to the underworld (Ishtar, Odysseus, Plato's Er) exhibit certain structural parallels to this model of ascent. The cosmic traveler is shown the workings of the world beyond death and returns to report his or her findings. So one could argue that the journey (even though a journey "down") functions to lend authority to the report. But there is one crucial difference. When one is taken to the highest heaven in texts of this type, one enters where no mortal belongs, while a journey to the underworld is the very opposite; it is where all are going.

I would attribute the fair number of Jewish (and Jewish-Christian) texts, in which heavenly ascent is a means of receiving revelation, to the "politics and piety" in and around the Second Temple period. Various groups are attempting to legitimate rival claims of revelation and authority. Given the Hebrew Bible traditions regarding the ascent of Enoch or Elijah, and the throne visions of Moses, Isaiah, Daniel or Ezekiel, one can trace an ongoing process of pseudepigraphal elaboration in which speculative lore receives grounding in the claimed revelations of such heroes. On the whole, this model of ascent, like my first, is relatively rare. In most Ancient Near Eastern and archaic Greek materials deities characteristically encounter humans through an epiphany or an oracle. The examples I have surveyed illustrate an emerging motif that spreads and is fundamentally transformed.

3. *Ascent to Heavenly Immortality*

I turn now to what one might call a "one-way" ascent, in contrast to the "round-trip" journey from earth, to heaven, and back again. I will focus on those cases where a mortal obtains immortality (or release from mortal conditions) through a final or permanent ascent to the heavenly realms. Broadly, this involves two overlapping ideas, both of which have been extensively investigated.[67]   First, that a hero, ruler, or extraordinary individual has obtained immortal heavenly existence.   Second, the more general idea that the souls of humankind, bound by mortal conditions, can obtain an immortal heavenly life.   The second should not be viewed as simply a later democratization of the first.   The two exist side by side throughout the Hellenistic period.   While they are distinct from one another, both are related to the fundamental shift in the perception of human place which I have described above.

The concept of divinity in this period is complex and many faceted.   To distinguish ancient theory (much less legend or gossip) from cultic fact is often impossible (as any reading of writers such as Diodorus, Plutarch, Pausanias, or Diogenes Laertius will quickly demonstrate).   At all times the historian must consider the various indigenous categories and points of reference which form the context in which discussions and debates about "divine" status make sense.[68]   In keeping with Guthrie's general rubric, (i.e., gods are immortal; humans are mortal), for the Greeks at least, to be immortal (*athanatos*) in any sense, *is* to be a god.[69]   But besides the Olympian and Chthonic deities, there were many humans who obtained some kind of divine/immortal status, in popular legend, folklore, literature and politics. Some are well-known and international in reputation (Herakles), while others are obscure or local.   And there were many ways in which mortals were believed to have been deified: through descent while still "alive" into the underworld (Amphiaraus, Trophonius); through transport to an earthly Paradise (Menelaus); through a special diet (Tantalus); through seizure and translation (Ganymede); through fiery purgation.[70]   But often, such "immortalization" involved some idea of ascent to heaven.   Whether one is thinking of an ancient hero or "demigod" such as Herakles,   a co-called "divine man" like Apollonius of Tyana, a deified philosopher such as Empedokles, a "Son of God" like Jesus, or the divine honors paid to Hellenistic kings and Roman emperors--this same basic idea is present: a mortal has achieved immortality.[71]   But this idea of special apotheosis needs to be seen in the context of the more general perception that all human souls are immortal, and thus divine, and that the proper goal of human life is to escape the bonds of mortality, whether earth or body, and ascend to heaven.

According to Cumont, the first precisely dated reference to astral immortality is by Aristophanes in 421 B.C.E.   In *Peace* (831) he greets the apparition of a new star as the Pythagorean poet Ion of Chios, who had recently died. He asks ironically whether it is true that "when someone dies, he becomes like the stars in the air."[72]   The origin and history of this idea is complex and obscure.[73]   The well-known golden *lamellai ("Golden Plates")*, found in tombs in Crete, Thessaly and Italy provide the most fascinating early evidence (4th century B.C.E.).   It appears that they were placed in the hand of the dead to remind the soul of the words to be used when facing the chthonic powers of the underworld, thus assuring a blessed state. One from Petelia, dated 350 B.C.E. reads:

> You will find to the left of the house of Hades a spring,
> And by its side, a white cypress.
> To this spring approach not near.
> But you shall find another, from the Lake of Memory
> Cold water flowing forth, but guards before it.
> Say, "*I am a child of Earth and starry Heaven;*
> *But my race is of Heaven alone.* This you know.
> But I am parched with thirst, I am perishing,
> Give me quickly the cold water flowing from
> the Lake of Memory!"
> And of themselves they will give you to drink of
> the holy spring;
> And then you will have lordship among the other heroes.[74]

It appears that those who composed and used these texts believed in some dualistic notion of a mortal body and an immortal soul, and sought to escape death by returning to heaven, the true home of the soul.[75] By Roman imperial times variations of this belief flourished, within the context of the new cosmology.[76] I have already quoted portions from "Scipio's Dream," in Cicero's *Republic*, which typify this idea of the ascent to the soul at death.

Jewish sources adopt and adapt both aspects of this notion of ascent to heavenly immortality. The complex development of views of the afterlife and apotheosis in Jewish circles around the Second Temple period has been extensively documented.[77] I have already mentioned the legends which grow up around Enoch and Elijah, who are special cases in the archaic period. As early as Maccabean times, Daniel speaks of the resurrected righteous as shining "like the stars forever and ever" (12:3). Some idea of ascent to heaven might well be implied here. Jesus is taken up bodily to heaven according to Luke (Acts 1:9-11). Paul's belief that the believers in Christ, both dead and living, will ascend to meet Jesus in the air, becoming in the process, "immortalized," illustrates the complex mixture of ideas in this period--resurrection of the body, ascent to heaven, mortals becoming immortal.

Of course there are significant differences between the *special apotheosis* of an extraordinary mortal (whether hero, magician, philosopher, savior, or ruler) and the idea that anyone and everyone is at least *potentially* immortal, i.e., can escape the bonds of mortality and ascend to heaven at death. I have grouped these together for two reasons. First, I would relate both to the fundamental shift in the perception of "human place" that I have described. With few exceptions, both phenomena are in sharp contrast to the archaic understanding of human mortality. Broadly speaking, it is in this new context that both notions are able to spread and flourish. The distinctions between the two are often blurred. At Augustus' funeral, according to Dio, Tiberius compared his father to Herakles and said, "It is fitting that we should not mourn for him, but while now *giving his body back to nature, should forever glorify his soul as a god.*"[78] When his body was consumed on the pyre, the senator Numerius Atticus swore that he had seen the emperor's soul ascending to heaven (for which Livia paid him a fee of one million sesterces!). After five days his *bones were placed in the tomb.* Here we have a clear recognition of bodily mortality, the idea of the immortal soul, and the notion of apotheosis of an extraordinary individual, all lumped together. Second, what happens to the extraordinary individual or hero often becomes the model for the devotees. Jonathan Smith, in commenting on the *Prayer of Joseph*, concludes:

> Thus the PJ takes its place among a host of texts witnessing to what I have come to believe is *the* fundamental [new] pattern of hellenistic Mediterranean religions--an astrological mystery involving the descent-ascent of a heavenly figure, the *Himmelreise der Seele* of the believer through the astral-angelic spheres and magical-theurgic practices.[79]

The success of the descending-ascending heavenly figure in moving through the astral spheres is related to the anticipated ascent of the believer. It might be argued that Smith's observation applies mainly to later gnostic systems of salvation, but that would be to isolate gnosticism as a particular religious manifestation, largely unconnected to what is generally going on among most "hellenistic Mediterranean religions" during this period. I would add to Smith's observation that the descending-ascending figure could well be only an "ascending" one. I don't think that the idea of heavenly preexistence is an absolute prerequisite to the general pattern he is describing. Of course this can get quite complicated, as Paul's Jesus well illustrates. As I pointed out in my second chapter, Paul may not have seen Jesus as a preexistent divine being. So we could call him an "ascending" savior figure, a mortal become immortal. Yet Paul does think he has battled with the various hostile powers of the heavenly spheres, so his ascent was not an "easy" one. And he also believes Jesus will *return* from heaven, presumably passing successfully through those same spheres. So there we do have a descent. And after collecting together the immortalized believers, there is apparently to be some type of ascent again, because Paul thinks that Jesus and his followers will finally conquer these hostile angelic forces. So you might say that Jesus is an ascending-descending-ascending heavenly figure (And, I might point out, if Paul expects some special apotheosis in his own case, before the return of Jesus from heaven, then presumably he too will become the same.). In the Gospel of John, Jesus is presented as the descending-ascending divine Son of God, who was sent from heaven and has returned to God (John 3:16; 16:18), while at the same time his disciples are promised a similar ascent to heaven (14:1-3). There seems to be a sense in which they too are "gods" (10:33-36).[80]

I want to relate this notion of final ascent to immortality to the more general belief that *mortals can escape the bonds of mortality.* This would include some of the more specific ways of speaking of such a release: whether ascent of the soul at death; bodily assumption (presumably in some transformed state); or resurrection of the body and ascent to heaven (again, presumably in some transformed state), and so forth. This type of ascent is in sharp contrast to my first two, neither of which contains the essential idea that heaven is the potential place for mortals to dwell. Since Paul believes that Jesus has ascended to the right hand of God; that he will possibly do the same before the end; that all believers, living and dead, will likewise be taken up at the end; we are obviously dealing with an understanding of ascent here that is essential to his religious system. But this is not the kind of heavenly journey he reports in 2 Cor. 12:1-10. That belongs in my fourth category.

4. Ascent as a Foretaste of the Heavenly World

In contrast to the previous type these are accounts of an ascent which is temporary or "round-trip." What distinguishes this from my first two categories, which were also ascent-descent journeys, is that the experience functions to some degree *as a foretaste or anticipation of a final or permanent ascent.* What the seer beholds and even experiences in some cases, mirrors what is expected at the end (whether end of life, history or whatever). My second category, ascent to receive revelation, obviously includes accounts in which the seer was shown the secrets of the heavenly world. What is the difference then between a "foretaste" of the heavenly world and a "revelation" thereof?   What one finds is a blending of the two models, an extension or augmentation of what I have argued is fundamentally archaic, in the light of a new cosmological perspective. Although both types do involve "revelation" in that sense, I think there is still a significant difference. When Isaiah sees the glory of the heavenly world and is before God's throne, the vision serves to validate his call and commission.   There is no idea that he somehow belongs in heaven rather than on earth, or that he is to return there someday. He is a mortal, clearly out of place, and making a once-and-for-all visit. But in many texts this is not the case; the privileged heavenly journey is proleptic in some sense. I would want to carefully qualify this, because there are texts which I would tend to place in this category, which do not emphasize this idea of a later final ascent.[81] But many do, and I think these can be clearly distinguished from the other three types I have surveyed.

First I want to examine tales and narratives of legendary figures. Then I will look at some materials that seem more closely related to an actual practice or experience of ascent, in an effort to move toward Paul's account, our only autobiographical example.

There are a number of tales that seem to go back to Plato's "Myth of Er" in *Republic* 10. 613D-21D. Plato relates how Er, slain in battle, returns to his body after twelve days and reports on his journey through the cosmos, having been shown the fate of souls after death.[82] I have already mentioned how Cicero models his account of Scipio's dream after this story. The ascent experience of Scipio is obviously proleptical. He sees and experiences what is expected to happen at the final ascent of the soul at death. He is caught up in what he sees, and in the very dream experiences a detachment from all that is earthly and mortal. He is admonished *even as he ascends*, to fix all his attention on the heavenly world. So there is a kind of conversion that goes on in the text itself (*Republic* 6. 16-19). It is this combination of the didactic and the experiential which gives the text such a dramatic flavor. Plutarch, in his work "On the Delays of Divine Vengeance," (*Moralia* 563B-68) tells of one Aridaius, who falls from a height, is "dead" for three days, and miraculously revives at the time of his own funeral. He experiences a total change in his way of life and relates to his friends how his soul was carried into the heavenly regions. Led by a guide, who declares that he is no longer to be called Aridaius, but Thespesius, he is shown the various fates of the souls of the dead. Like Plato, Plutarch uses the tale as a literary device within a philosophical discussion on divine punishment. He tells another story about Timarchus, who similarly returns to life after two nights and a day, having made a journey through the cosmos ("On the Sign of Socrates" *Moralia* 590-92). Both stories are related to the kind of cosmological specula- tions and discussions found in his "Concerning the Face of the Moon" (*Moralia* 920-54). This whole genre is in turn related to the more archaic journeys to the underworld, except that now the trip through the cosmos can show a way of escaping the lower mortal world and ascending to heaven.

In Jewish and Christian circles there is a complicated development of as- cent traditions around such figures as Enoch, Abraham, Moses, Elijah, Isaiah, Peter, Paul and John. Many of our texts which report the ascent of these figures make use of the type of guided tour journey. I have already noted in the *Book of the Watchers* how the heavenly traveler is taken through the levels of heaven, shown eschatological and cosmological secrets, and finally is brought before the throne of God. But in many cases the ascent is proleptic. What the figure sees and experiences is related to his expectations of a return ascent, and often that of the community as well. The tradition serves to validate the expectations of the group which creates or uses the text.

The *Similitudes of Enoch* (*1 Enoch* 37-71), possibly dating from the first century C.E., records the visionary journeys of Enoch into the heavenly realms.[83] In chapter 39, which is part of the first "Parable" (chapters 38-44), Enoch relates how he was taken to heaven:

> And in those days a whirlwind carried me off
> from the earth,
> And set me down at the end of the heavens.
> And there I saw another vision, the dwelling-places
> of the holy,
> And the resting-places of the righteous.
> Here mine eyes saw their dwellings with
> His righteous angels,
> And their resting-places with the holy.[84]

In the same place he sees the "Elect One" who dwells under the wings of the Lord of Spirits (39:6a-7a).[85]

He then says:

> And the righteous shall prevail in his days,
> And the righteous and elect shall be without number
> before Him forever and ever.
> And all the righteous and elect before him
> *shall shine as fiery lights*
> And their mouth shall be full of blessing (39:6b-7b).

Enoch is overcome with the splendor and glory which he sees before the throne. He declares:

> There I wished to dwell,
> And my spirit *longed for* that
> dwelling place (39:8).

He is given assurance that he will obtain his heavenly destiny and for a long time he beholds the throne of God while reciting hymns and blessings. His chanting seems to reach a climax when he experiences a transformation:

> *And my face was changed*;
> for I could no longer behold (39:14).

This extraordinary text epitomizes the model of proleptic ascent. It is clear throughout this section of *1 Enoch* that the "elect and righteous" are destined for heavenly glory. Of the wicked, in contrast, it is declared: "And into heaven they shall *not* ascend!" (45:2). The elect will shine like stars and be clothed with garments of glory (62:15). So Enoch's experience of ascent to the throne of God functions as a revelation of the heavenly life the elect will enjoy, while at the same time it is a *foretaste* of the final ascent of Enoch himself. Chapter 70 reports this final ascent; he is taken up "during his lifetime" and joins the righteous who dwell in the heavenly place he had visited before. Chapter 71 is difficult. As it now stands it appears to be an elaboration of Enoch's translation mentioned in chapter 70. But it might possibly be a second version of his previous ascent, parallel to chapter 39.[86] The account begins:

> And it came to pass after this that my spirit
> was translated,
> And it ascended into the heavens:
> And I saw the holy sons of God.

> They were stepping on flames of fire:
> Their garments were white,
> And their faces shone like snow (71:1).

Michael the archangel is Enoch's guide. He shows him "all the secrets of the ends of heaven" and his spirit is further translated "into the heaven of heavens" (71:4-5). God, who is called the "Head of Days," actually comes out of his palace, escorted by his angels, to welcome Enoch (71:9-10). Enoch is overcome as he beholds the indescribable glory of God:

> And I fell on my face,
> And my whole body became relaxed,
> And *my spirit was transfigured*;
> And I cried with a loud voice,
> . . . with the spirit of power,
> And blessed and glorified and
> extolled (71:11).

At this point there is a break in the text; it appears in verses 14-17 that Enoch is declared to be the "Son of Man" (or a "son of man"), which might imply some kind of exalted or divine status.[87] I am inclined to see this chapter as an account of Enoch's final translation, an alternative version of 70:1-4. Yet it parallels chapter 39 in a striking manner. As the accounts now stand in this section of *1 Enoch* 37-71, the initial journey anticipates the final transformation and exaltation described in chapter 71. The *Similitudes* contains additional material, typical of this genre, such as astronomical secrets, eschatological revelations, and the names and functions of angels. But this text *moves beyond* this archaic idea of ascent as a cosmic tour (i.e., ascent as a mode of revelation) and becomes a proleptic journey, an anticipation of final heavenly glory.

The text known as *2 (Slavonic) Enoch*, dating from the first century C.E., shares some basic similarities with this section of the *Similitudes*.[88] It reports how two angels appear to Enoch, carrying him up through the seven heavens where he sees the Lord, sitting on a high throne (chapters 1-20). On the way up he is shown the cosmic secrets of each level of heaven. The angels leave him in the seventh heaven, since they are not permitted to approach any closer to the throne. Then Gabriel himself, one of the chief angels, lifts him up higher and places him before the Lord's face (21:5). The Lord declares, "Let Enoch step up to stand before my face into eternity," to which the angelic servants reply, "Let him step up." At this point Enoch is transformed:

> And the Lord said to Michael: "Go take Enoch from out of his earthly garments, and anoint him with my sweet ointment, and put *garments of glory*." And Michael did thus, as the Lord told him. He anointed me, and dressed me, and the appearance of that ointment is more than the great light, and his ointment is like the sweet dew and its smell mild, singing like the sun's ray,

> and *I looked at myself, and was like one of his glorious ones, and there was no difference* (22:8-10, recension A).

It should be noted here that Enoch's garments are *already* before the throne of God, awaiting him. This should be compared to Paul's description of the future glorification of the mortal body in 2 Cor. 5:1-10 (also cf. *Ascension of Isaiah* 7:22). This astounding scene of exaltation and glorification is followed by the revelation of "all things" to Enoch. For thirty days and thirty nights he writes down these revelations, filling 360 books (23:1-6). The remaining chapters of *2 Enoch* (24-66) appear to relate some of these cosmic secrets revealed to him. His heavenly journey lasts 60 days (68:1-3, recension A), whereupon he returns to earth for thirty days, hands the heavenly books over to his sons, and is taken up to heaven again in a *final ascent*. Between his two ascents, it is as though he has already become "heavenly"--he tells his son Methosalam:

> Hear child, from the time when the Lord anointed me with the ointment of his glory, there has been no food in me, and my soul remembers not earthly enjoyment, neither do I want anything earthly (56:2, recension A).

These characteristics: not wanting food or anything earthly, knowing "all things" (cf. Gen. 3:22); having a transformed face (37:2) and not needing to sleep (23:3), are those of a divine being.

Although *2 Enoch* focuses on the extraordinary experience of Enoch, throughout the book heavenly glorification is promised to the righteous. God has prepared "many mansions" for them, they will "be eternal and incorruptible," shining forth "more than the sun sevenfold" (61:2; 65:8; 66:7-8). Ascent, in this text, is a way of claiming heavenly authority for the revelations the book contains. But Enoch's initial journey to heaven functions as a proleptic realization of the glorification and exaltation that comes when he is finally taken up. At the same time *his* ascent has an explicit relationship with the more general promise to heavenly life for all the elect.

The *Ascension of Isaiah*, sections of which are dated to the first and second centuries C.E., focuses even more explicitly on this idea of ascent as a foretaste of heavenly glory.[89] In 6:1-11:4, which is of Christian origin, the text expands the vision of Isa. 6:1-13 into a full-scale account of the prophet's ascent through the seven heavens and his appearance before the throne of God. As Isaiah is taken up through the first five levels, he sees in each a glorious figure seated on a throne, surrounded by bands of angels offering praise to God. Each level surpasses the previous one in glory and they are separated by great distances. The drama of the ascent is heightened as he moves closer and closer to God's throne. He is so overcome by the splendor and glory of the second heaven that he ignorantly falls down before the throne in that level, thinking he has seen God. He is rebuked by his escort:

> Worship neither angel nor throne which belongs to the six
> heavens--for this reason I was sent to conduct you--till I tell you
> in the seventh heaven (7:21).

He is then given an extraordinary promise:

> For above all the heavens and their angels is *your throne set, and
> your garments and your crown* which you shall see (7:22).

As with Enoch, his glorification and rule is assured, already in heaven.
He interprets this as a promise that would include *all* the faithful:

> And I rejoiced greatly that those who love the Most High
> and his Beloved [Christ] will *at their end ascend here* by
> the angel of the Holy Spirit (7:23).

As Isaiah ascends from heaven to heaven, his face is gradually transformed,
becoming more glorious (7:25). The text reflects a sense of greater and
greater distance from the world below (7:24). In the sixth heaven the extraordinary uniqueness of the journey is emphasized:

> But I say to you, Isaiah, that *no one* who has to return to a body
> in this world *has ascended or seen or perceived what you have and
> what you will yet see*, for it is appointed to you in the lot of the
> Lord to come up here. And I extolled my Lord with praise that I
> through his lot should come up here (8:11-13).

Here the author of the text shows that he has in mind two types of ascent, a
permanent or final one, and this rare and privileged visit. At this level the
light and splendor of all the previous heavens seem dark by comparison, and
he begins to hear sounds of praise that are different as well (8:20-21). He is
fully persuaded that he has reached the ultimate level and wants to remain
there, never returning to the earth. He is told:

> If you rejoice already in this light, how much will you rejoice
> when, in the seventh heaven, you see that light where God and
> his Beloved are, from where I have been sent (8:25).

> As far as your wish not to return to the flesh is concerned, you
> days are not yet fulfilled that you may come here (8:27)

As he finally approaches the seventh heaven there is a sense of danger, a
voice cries out, "How far shall he ascend who dwells among aliens?" Here we
have a perfect example of the archaic idea of ascent as an invasion. Isaiah is
afraid and trembles, then another voice cries out, "It is permitted to the holy

Isaiah to ascend here, for his garment is here" (9:1-2). In other words, *he* is not truly an alien, but does belong in heaven. So for him the ascent is not an invasion. In the seventh heaven he sees Abel and Enoch and all the righteous from the time of Adam, clothed in garments of glory like the angels, but not having yet received their crowns (9:6-10). These are reserved until the sending of Christ to the earth and his return from heaven. When Isaiah finally sees the Son of God and begins to praise him, along with all the hosts of heaven, *he is totally transformed*, becoming glorious like the angels (9:28-30). He sees and hears the future: that the Son of God will descend to earth, be crucified, resurrected, and return to heaven. The text closes by relating that Isaiah delivered this secret revelation to king Hezekiah and that Satan had the prophet sawed in half on because of his ascent.

This text is paradigmatic of the model as a whole. It contains the following elements:

1. A mortal is taken up to the highest heaven

2. The ascent is an extraordinary privilege

3. The way is fraught with danger and can only be successfully undertaken through divine permission and power

4. There is great distance between the earthly and heavenly realms with increasing beauty and splendor (or danger for the uninvited) as one moves up, and an increasing sense of alienation from the world below

5. The ascent itself is a transforming experience in which the candidate is progressively glorified

6. The climax of the journey is an encounter with the highest god

7. One is given secret revelations, or shown mysteries

8. The ascent is followed by a return to the world below to live on as a mortal

9. What is seen and heard can be selectively passed on to those who are worthy

10. The one who has ascended faces the opposition of lower spiritual powers upon his return.

I have isolated these elements as a general way of setting forth an expanded set of perceptions about this type of ascent. Obviously not every text will contain all of these, nor will any given text necessarily be limited to them. But it is a useful list, and provides a way to do comparisons.

THINGS UNUTTERABLE: PAUL'S ASCENT TO PARADISE

There are definite links between the language and ideas of these Jewish and Jewish-Christian ascent traditions, developed around legendary figures from Israel's history, and the Tannaitic and Amoraic *Merkabah* traditions (as well as the later *Hekhalot* literature).[90] The question of how the exegetical character of the *Merkabah* materials is linked to mystical experience or practice is unresolved; and conversely, the issue of links between the later *Hekhalot* texts, which are directly tied to visionary experiences, and the earlier exegetical traditions, is likewise unclear. As an example of a later text that seems closely related to an actual practice of ascent, I will briefly examine *Hekhalot Rabbati*.[91]

This text, perhaps dating from as early as the third century C.E., is a diverse collection of materials, mostly attributed to R. Ishmael, and related to Jewish speculations about the heavenly world and the throne God. Indeed its goal is the vision of the *merkabah*, the divine throne "chariot" of God (Ezekiel 1, 10). It contains a rather detailed account of ascent through the seven heavens to God's throne (chapters 15-25). The journey can be quite dangerous and is only to be undertaken by one who is "worthy," one pure in all the virtues and observant of the whole Torah (15:1-2; 20:4; text references follow Wertheimer's edition). There are seven palaces (temples of heaven), each of which is guarded by eight angelic gatekeepers (17:1-8). The mystic must master all their names, calling upon Surya, the Angel of the Presence 112 times to protect him from each of them as he ascends and descends (16:4-5). At each gate "seals" are shown to the guardians, and the initiate, if allowed to go on, is "sent forth with glory" to the next level (19:1-5). Passage through the sixth palace is especially dangerous; the guards will destroy any who seek to go up higher without permission (19:6). After satisfying certain requirements at this level, the mystic is taken past the gate of the seventh palace to appear before God's throne:

> Then they take him before the throne of glory. They go before him with all kinds of music and song until *they lift him up and seat him near the cherubim*, by the Wheels, near to the holy living creatures. He beholds marvels, powers, splendor, greatness, holiness, purity, terror, meekness and righteousness--all at the same time (22:2).

The text continues with a number of appended sections, including a second scene in which the initiate presents himself before the throne of glory (24:1-5). This reception is rather astounding. Not only does the initiate gaze upon the throne of God, but he is welcomed into the divine court, is alternatively seated and/or presented before God, and participates in the round of chanting and praising that goes on continually before the throne.

What seems to be the point of such an ascent? The text says a few things about this. The mystic testifies of the awesome glory of God, which far surpasses anything that can be seen "in the palaces of flesh and blood" below (18:3). He returns to tell "the seed of Abraham" what he has seen and heard

(18:5). God apparently delights in this whole activity, waiting for the arrival of each faithful one, willingly sharing these secret and hidden things with those worthy (18:3; 22:3). But is there any further point? Gershom Scholem concluded that in this material "the ecstatic sees in his lifetime what other people see only after death . . . ."[92] But he based this very general conclusion on a whole series of texts which he simply grouped together (*Hekhalot* literature; some of the bits and pieces of *merkabah* material in *b. Hagigah* 12-15 and elsewhere; *2 Enoch*; Paul's text in 2 Cor. 12:2-4; *Testament of Levi*; Clement's quotation from the lost *Apocalypse of Zephania*). Can this conclusion be supported in the case of *Hekhalot Rabbati*? The text, as it now stands, does have some interest in calculating the time of the end, with three apocalyptic prose sections in the first part (chapters 1-12), but this material seems unrelated to the practice of ascent. There is a stray reference to the seer hearing of "the salvation of the end" (18:5). But the text itself gives no hint of what might have been expected in connection with any such "end." There seems to be nothing explicit beyond this. Still, I would include it under this category of ascent as a foretaste of the heavenly world. I think Scholem's point stands. Generally speaking, the *extended merkabah* tradition develops in a context which includes ideas about "the world to come," punishments of the wicked, eternal life for the righteous, and different levels of blessedness in the heavenly world (Paradise). The archaic notion of death as the end, or a shadowy life in Sheol (which the Sadducees apparently maintained), does not predominate in Jewish circles into our era. It would seem that a text like *Hekhalot Rabbati* should be read with that more general context in mind. But perhaps more important is the climax of the ascent in this text, where the initiate is *enthroned* in the heavenly court. The way he is welcomed, the intimacy with God, the exaltation, all point to something more. As a mortal, he is dwelling out of his place, but there is no danger, he has been *received*. That he can successfully go up and return at will, and "no creature will stop him" (23:3) seems to imply he has met all tests of judgment (personal piety, keeping the Torah, knowledge of secret magical lore) and therefore has cosmically conquered. That this would imply a similar reception at death is likely. Regardless, I have included it here because of its connections to this earlier ascent material that focuses on legendary figures. It shows that Jews had more than a literary or exegetical interest in the idea of the heavenly journey with its goal of seeing the mysteries of the throne of God. Throughout the period, and here Paul is our firsthand example, various individuals claimed to have actually experienced such trips.

To conclude my discussion of this model of ascent I will move outside this Jewish provenance to examine three additional texts which also seem to be tied to some actual experience of ascent.

In Apuleius' *Metamorphoses* there is an account of ascent in connection with the initiation drama of the Isis cult. This account of Lucius' initiation has been thoroughly examined by scholars and it appears to offer a fair reflection of the spiritual mood and ritual details involved in such a process.[93] Book 11 opens with a moving account of Lucius' conversion to the goddess Isis, when "weary of all cruel fortune and calamity," she appears to him in all her splendor and power (11. 3-6). He is overcome at her beauty and graciousness and she addresses him:

> Lo, I am with you Lucius, moved by your prayers, I who am the mother of the universe, the mistress of all the elements, the first offspring of time, the highest of deities, the queen of the dead, foremost of heavenly beings, the single form that fuses all gods and goddesses; *I who order by my will the starry heights of heaven*, the health-giving breezes of the sea, and the *awful silences of those in the underworld*; my single godhead is adored by the whole world in varied forms, in differing rites and with many diverse names.[94]

Through her grace he is released from hostile Fate and transformed from an ass (which he had become through evil magic) to a man (11. 13-15). Lucius devotes himself totally to service of the goddess, continually receiving from her "visions and counsel," and longing for the day when he will be allowed to undergo the secret initiation of the cult. Finally, his great moment arrives, and Apuleius offers the reader of the novel an altogether tantalizing account of what was involved in the initiation (11. 23). The priest escorts Lucius to the baths for the customary ablution, then takes him to a room in a temple, placing him before the image of the goddess and giving him "certain secret instructions too holy to be uttered." After a ten day fast he is taken alone into another room, clothed in a new garment of linen and there the initiation experience transpires. What took place, we are told, is *unlawful to tell* (recall Paul's statement about his ascent, 2 Cor. 12:2-4), but as curious readers we are offered the following cryptic description:

> I approached the boundary of death and treading on Proserpine's threshold, I was carried through all the elements, after which I returned. At dead of night I saw the sun flashing with bright effulgence. I approached close to the gods above and the gods below and worshiped them face to face (11. 23).

Every conceivable hypothesis as to what might have been involved in this experience has been suggested. Was it some kind of a mystical drama acted out for the initiate? Could it have been a certain trance state induced by drugs or magical means? Was it a revelation of certain secret doctrines of the cult? Every phrase of the description is problematic. The line *accessi confinium mortis et calcato Proserpinae limine* ("I approached the boundary of death and treading on Proserpine's threshold"), seems to indicate that the initiate enters the underworld, the realm of the dead.[95] Perhaps, in accordance with Egyptian funerary ideas, there is an identity here with Osiris, whose body remained in the underworld while his soul was taken up by Re, the sun god, in his daily cycle from the heavens, through the underworld and back.[96] The reference to travel *per omnia vectus elementa* ("I was carried through all the elements") could well meann a journey through the planetary spheres.[97] To see the sun flashing brightly *nocta media* ("at dead of night") seems to indicate again some notion of the underworld, perhaps that the sun revives and glorifies the dead. The beholding of the *deos inferos et deos superos* ("the gods above and the gods below") might refer to chthonian deities, but more likely, since Isis presides over the whole cosmos, to the entire divine realm of heaven, earth and underworld.[98] Although no interpretation of this text can be certain, I am inclined to see it as a description of a descent-ascent journey through the whole cosmos. The report breaks down into four statements. The first two give an overview of the entire cosmic journey:

1. I approached the boundary of death and treading on Proserpine's threshold ... (underworld)

2. I was carried through all the elements, after which I returned (planetary spheres)

The traveler has gone from earth, to the underworld, up through the heavens and returned to earth. The third statement adds further explanation about being in the underworld, perhaps implying that though entering death's realm there was an awakening. The fourth summarizes the point of the whole journey--intimacy with all the powers of the cosmos:

3. At dead of night I saw the sun flashing with bright effulgence (underworld)

4. I approached close to the *gods above and the gods below* and worshiped them face to face (whole cosmos)

The pattern of the experience fits the model of death-resurrection-ascension. The term *renatus* (rebirth) occurs in 11. 16 and 11. 21, and following the initiation there is a reference to *natalem sacrorum* (11. 24), so it is a birth from the dead, an concept known to us from Christian sources. In Rev. 1:5 Jesus is called "firstborn from the dead," and in 1:18, as a glorified heavenly being declares, ". . . I died, and behold I am alive for evermore, and I have the keys of Death and Hades [i.e., the lower world]."[99]

Following the initiation Lucius is brought out of the room and he stands on a platform adorned like the statue of Isis while the crowd of worshipers gathers around to behold him (11. 24). Since it is Isis who orders the starry heights of heaven *and* the awful silences of the underworld, I have interpreted the experience as a journey through her cosmic realm in which one greets all the gods face to face. This is the crucial focus of the text. To know and name all the powers in a *positive* way is to be released from Fate and death. Although the inclusion of the underworld reflects a more archaic cosmological structure, this initiation journey is nonetheless proleptic, offering the candidate a foretaste or guarantee of blessedness beyond. In her initial revelation Isis had promised Lucius:

91

> You shall live indeed a happy man, you shall live full of glory
> in my protection, and when you have completed the span of
> your lifetime, you will pass down to the nether world, but here
> also, in the very midst of the subterranean hemisphere, you shall
> often worship me, whom you now see, as one who favors you,
> shining in the darkness of Acheron and ruling in the Stygian
> depth, when you all the while shall dwell in the Elysian fields.
> But if with diligent service, religious tendance and constant
> chastity you will be worthy of my godhead, know that I alone
> have power to prolong your life also beyond the span deter-
> mined by your destiny (11.6).

The terms used here for the afterlife are drawn from standard Greek eschatology, and as in the Homeric Hades, the "darkness of Acheron" and the "Stygian depths" refer to the underworld. Homer and Hesiod place Elysium or the "Isles of the Blessed" at the ends of the earth. It could be, since Isis is the speaker here, that to dwell in the Elysian fields is to escape the power of death and obtain some type of celestial life beyond.[100] After all, in this text the highlight of the initiation experience seems to be the greeting of the gods *above* as well as below. I have included it here, despite its more archaic cosmological vocabulary, because it nonetheless illustrates the pattern of proleptic ascent. In this case the language of direction (i.e., "up" or "down") is subordinate to that of relationship. One either either descends to the "awful silences" of the underworld, or is in the hands of the goddess, so that essentially, we are dealing with a contrast between death and immortality.

In the Hermetic text *Poimandres*, the journey "up" seems to become a journey *within*. The text opens with a visionary epiphany in which the god Poimandres appears to the seeking disciple, revealing to him a message of salvation (1. 1-3).[101] As the vision unfolds there is no real emphasis on *external* movement, and there are almost no ritual details. The journey seems to be a "looking within", whereby the disciple "travels" up or out by entering into himself, i.e., into his own mind (*nous*). There is a repeated play on the word *nous*, which is understood to be a reflection of the macrocosm. Poimandres, the god, is Mind/Nous, as seen in the "*egō Nous*" confession early on in the vision (1. 6). But there are references by the disciple to "*Nous ho emos*" or to "*nous emos*" (my *nous*), which seem to refer at the same time to the Mind-God Poimandres as well (1. 16, 21). The disciples is told, "Hold in your mind (*nous*) whatever you want to learn" (1. 3); then he sees "in his mind" or "in the Mind" the revelation of the origins of all things (1. 7, 8). As a human, he has the *Nous* of the Father, and only needs to look within (1. 6). One gets the sense that Poimandres is not really revealing anything to the disciple, but rather guiding him to recognize what he *already knows* (see 1. 20). Salvation involves the same kind of self-recognition experienced in the vision itself (1. 21). At the end he writes down the good news Poimandres has revealed *in himself* (1. 30). I have interpreted this vision as a journey because the experience becomes a proleptic realization of the final ascent in which one rises up at death through the seven planetary spheres to God. This final journey *is* presented in the text as external movement up (the *anodos* of 1. 24-26). The vision unfolds dynamically, as something progressively experienced rather than merely revealed or proclaimed. Here is an example of how an older structure with its language (that of ascent as external movement up) can be taken over and used in a different way. To journey within, to see and experience one's true self, i.e., the god within, is to move from the earthly and mortal to the immortal and divine. The revelation itself is freedom and immortality (1. 28), and as such anticipates the final release and ascent at death.

Finally, I want to look at the so-called "Mithras Liturgy" as an example of a rather different kind of text.[102] It provides the initiate with a *guide* for making such a journey, relating how one can ascend, what will be seen and heard on the way, and what is to be done by the candidate at various points. In contrast to *Poimandres*, the text is full of ritual elements--amulets, magical formulas, breathing techniques, special recipes-- and the tone is far from calm or meditative. At the same time, these characteristics, which have often been classified as "magical," are combined with a profound expression of piety, worshipful adoration, wonder, and joy. This belies the oft-repeated misconception that magic is compulsion, in contrast to religion which is devotion. For example, at one point, in the first stages of the ascent, after completing a series of ritual utterances, the candidate is told:

> Then open your eyes, and you will see the doors open and the world of the gods which is within the doors, so that *from the pleasure and joy of the sight* your spirit runs ahead and ascends! (*PGM* 4. 624b-27).

The journey is more than a guided tour. The description is dynamic and quite complex; it seems to contain more than external movement. The move up involves an experience of transformation; it is a move between the mortal and divine realms. In the opening invocation one is to declare:

> For today I am about to behold, with immortal eyes--I born mortal from mortal womb, but transformed by tremendous power and an incorruptible right hand!--and with immortal spirit, the immortal Aion and master of the fiery diadems--I sanctified through holy consecrations!--while there subsists within me, holy, for a short time, my human soul-might, which I will again receive after the present necessity which is pressing down upon me . . . (*PGM* 4. 516-26).

As with *Poimandres*, the journey up seems to be fundamentally a journey within--inside the self, a beholding of the immortal nature beyond the bounds of mortality and Fate. The text reflects some sort of creation myth in the opening rituals, so that salvation in this text apparently involves a reversal of creation, an escape from the bonds of *anagkē*, a kind of cosmic

93

necessity or fate. There are references to *seeing oneself* (539), and to looking *within oneself* (629), and what appears to be a journey into one's own organs (576-629). At this point the ascent becomes very dangerous, with a near total loss of the self and the need for a protecting guide in order to go further (630-60). Whereas one had to disguise oneself earlier (570-75), here one experiences a breakthrough or crossing of a boundary--confessing one's *true* identity and greeting the powers of Fate in a *positive* way (630-93). Finally, one comes before the supreme God and receives a revelation (695-724). At this stage the candidate seems to hear with divine ears, in some sense *having undergone a kind of "death" or loss of self* (725-31). This "deification" (*apothantismos*--lines 740-45, 770-74) is an experience during one's lifetime, not after death, so one must return to the mortal realm. The ritual can be selectively passed on to others (730-50).

What I find particularly noteworthy in this text is that even though the candidate is to "ascend to heaven and behold all things" (484), after the beginning ritual in which he sees himself being "lifted up" (539), there is *no further language of external upward movement*. The passing through various levels or stages of "ascent" seems best understood as a movement within. The motif of the journey to heaven is taken over and becomes a *journey of transformation*. To go "up" is to go beyond, to cross the bounds of Fate and mortality and to see one's true self.

The text as we have it is addressed to a "daughter," and is a ritual for obtaining "immortalization" (475-480). This seems to be its original form and purpose.[103] It is later revised into a text for divination ("ask the god for what you want and he will give it to you" lines 475-76). In the main body, especially lines 720-734, one also receives a revelation. The opening lines (475-484) connect with the ending, mentioning the request for immortality and the special preparations of herbs and spices which are described at the end. But more important, the invocation (beginning with line 485) is a request for immortal birth, the power for a mortal to temporarily escape mortality through transformation and enter the world beyond. The text presupposes a complex cosmology, perhaps even a fall of some type, into the mortal world of birth and death. This is a most serious text, and it is unlikely that one goes through all this, finally coming before the most high god, only to ask some petty question. The revelation that is given is an oracle, and the recipient is told he will remember it later, even if it is thousands of verses long (lines 724-731). It could well have to do with the deification. Although the development of these magical traditions likely involved a number of stages, I see every reason to accept the version we have at face value, as a text that was preserved and used in its present form for its stated purpose--to obtain immortality. Since the candidate returns to the mortal realm, we can only assume that the experience of having already passed through all the powers of the cosmos and being received graciously by all the gods, would offer a way of return. The very idea of a mortal being promised, or somehow already having, immortality, seems to necessarily include some kind of final departure from the mortal world below. Yet, I admit the text tells us

94

little to nothing about such implications. The text does provide a valuable witness to an actual *practice* of ascent. The magical elements, the vivid descriptions of the heavenly powers, the sense of danger--all remind us that behind the literary descriptions of the journey to heaven was a serious enterprise.

Despite the important differences in the variety of texts I have just surveyed, I maintain that the basic idea of ascent to heaven as a foretaste of the heavenly world is a helpful categorical distinction. Such a journey anticipates a final ascent or heavenly destiny. It is an highly privileged experience. It often involves the reception of revelation, but is more than that, the journey itself functions as a proleptic "crossing the the bounds," a move from mortal to heavenly realms. As such, it can be an experience of transformation. It is something granted graciously to the initiate, thus beyond human power and often fraught with potential danger. It often culminates with a face to face encounter with the highest powers of the heavenly world.

In proposing my four models I have concentrated on the question of function. Most of the texts I have cited are literary reports, raising the question of the purpose of the author in drawing upon this particular motif. Alan Segal observes that the strategy underlying most all literary accounts of heavenly journeys in this period is "to guarantee and legitimate that heaven attests to the values which will be propounded in the document."[104] Other than the very earliest texts which see ascent negatively, as invasion, this certainly seems to be an important function in a long list of texts I have examined--Isa. 6:1-13, the *Book of the Watchers*, the *Testament of Levi*, Parmenides' *prooemium*, Cicero's report of Scipio's dream, Plutarch's various stories of returning from the dead, the *Similitudes of Enoch*, *2 Enoch*, the *Ascension of Isaiah*, and *Poimandres*--to name some of the more important examples. In the case of reports of the heavenly translation of a specific individual (my "final ascent" category), since the author is usually sympathetic to the figure, the account attests to the extraordinary career or divine approval of such a one (e.g., Diogenes Laertius' accounts of the end of Empedokles; Philostratus' treatment of Apollonius of Tyana; Luke's treatment of Jesus). Of course Lucian would be an exception to this when he draws upon the very same pattern to poke fun at such a character (as in *The Passing of Peregrinus*). I have tried to supplement Segal's observation by this attempt to classify these materials more specifically.

Practice and Provenance

At this point I want to try to move beyond the theoretical classification of these ascent texts to a more specific historical line of investigation. After all, we do have more than literary accounts, and in the case of Paul, firsthand testimony. What does this diverse material, literary or otherwise, tell us about any actual practice of ascent, or of any specific tradition?

In the case of our vast number of Jewish and Christian texts from Second Temple times, the evidence that various reports of visions and revelations are grounded in the experiences of the authors and/or preservers seems indisputable. The many references to dreams, to preparations such as fasting, special diet or drink, to special times, and to body posture, indicate familiarity with mystical techniques.[105] This seems also the case with the scattered references to the visionary experiences of the Rabbis in the literature of the Tannaim and Amoraim; though here, as Jacob Neusner, David Halperin, and others have shown, the textual tradition is complex and layered and one must use extreme caution in drawing conclusions about the early Palestinian rabbis. [106] Certainly the later *hekhalot* literature comes directly from the experiences of those who treasured and preserved it.

With reports such as those in Cicero or Plutarch, the evidence is less clear. We seem here to be dealing with literary creations modeled after Plato's tale of Er. Yet there is a rich tradition of Greek shamanistic materials obviously rooted in the practice and experience of various groups.[107] In the case of *Poimandres* we can safely assume that it reflects the visionary experience of the author(s).[108] Despite its very stylized form, there are indications in the text itself of liturgical/cultic activity (1. 29-31) and communal mission (1. 26b-28). Certainly Apuleius' account of the Isis initiation accurately reflects cultic practice.[109] The "Mithras Liturgy" is a rare witness, not only that ascent was practiced, but what preparations and techniques might have been involved. It reminds us that ritual practices (amulets, potions, secret formulas, sometimes pejoratively termed "magic") can function with personal piety and religious devotion within a highly complex theological system which has as its goal a transforming encounter with the highest deity.

What about historical links between these various texts? Scholem has demonstrated the antiquity of the tradition now preserved in the *Hekhalot* literature, linking it with older Jewish apocalyptic texts (e.g., *2 Enoch*, Testament of Levi, *Life of Adam and Eve*) and what he calls the "Gnosis of the Tannaitic Merkabah mystics."[110] Strugnell has published two fragments from an "angelic liturgy" found among the Qumran materials which appear to be related to the literary and conceptual background of the hymnological material in the *Hekhalot* traditions.[111] I would suggest that the passage in *War Scroll* (I QM 10:10-17) about seeing and hearing "profound things" might well be a reference to visionary experience. There seems to be a line (however thin) of "theosophic" tradition and practice running from the oldest Enoch material through later *Hekhalot* literature.[112] Scholem would place Paul right in the chronological center of this enterprise, precisely on the basis of his claim to have ascended to Paradise.[113] A focus on secret lore regarding the structure of the various heavens, the names of angels, and the vision of the throne of God lies at the heart of both the literary-exegetical and the practical-experiental development of this tradition, but that is about all one can say. To attempt precise historical linking is generally impossible given the complexity of this very diverse evidence. Various Jewish groups, for different reasons, at various times, in scattered places do reflect this general interest and focus.

Still, I would not want to isolate these texts of Jewish provenance from other Hellenistic ascent materials. Jean Daniélou and Robert Grant have shown that this kind of material runs through early Christian and "gnostic" texts[114]. In his important article on *Hekhalot Rabbati* Morton Smith points out the parallels between the Greek magical papyri (especially the "Mithras Liturgy"), the strands of similar esoteric tradition in Tannaitic texts, and the *Hekhalot* materials. He notes that how Scholem's study of the *hekhalot* traditions led him to conclusions amazingly close to those of Goodenough from his study of archaeological remains. He writes:

> It is impossible to deny the relationship of this material [i.e., Greek magical papyri] to the *hekhalot* tradition. The contrast between mortal and immortal beings, the ascent from the realm of mortality to that of the immortals, the jealous guards to be mastered by the use of magic names, the entrance of the heavenly realm, when the hostile gods all stare at the intruder, . . . all these characteristics are common to the Jewish and the magical material.[115]

He accounts for this by theorizing that ". . . the Hellenistic period saw the development of a Judaism profoundly shaped by Greco-Oriental thought, in which mystical and magical . . . elements were very important. From this common background such elements were derived independently by the magical papyri, Gnosticism, Christianity and Hellenistic and Rabbinic Judaism."[116]

Ironically, with all this material on ascent, stretching over hundreds of years, Paul's testimony of his own journey to Paradise is perhaps our *best* evidence that we are dealing with something that was practiced. Here we do have a case of a named and known individual who tells of his own experience. It is to that rare account that I will turn in the following chapter.

Conclusions

I have argued here that the Hellenistic idea of the heavenly journey is related to what Nilsson has called a "new cosmology." This notion of a move from the realm of the human and the mortal to that of the divine and the immortal is a fundamental characteristic of religions of the period. It has to do, first and foremost, with the perception of human place. That man is no longer at home on this earth, that he is subject to death and controlled by the powers of fate, that he is separated or has fallen) from the Divine--these are characteristic features of such a perception. Salvation then, is a reversal, an overcoming of the world, seen as flight and transformation. The idea of ascent is the most basic expression of that salvation. Whether seen as a journey up or a journey within, it involves an obtaining or recovery of man's true home, the realization of his heavenly destiny.

The idea of the journey to the realm of the divine before death, with a descent back to the earthly realm, functions within the context of this general understanding of human place. Such a move, like the epiphany of the god who comes down, is a means of revelation. But beyond that, it is often a foretaste of a final ascent, when one can return to the heavenly world, or otherwise escape the mortal bonds. One can stress both similarities and differences in this type of heavenly journey. As one must accurately speak of Hellenistic ways of salvation, one must recognize corresponding differences in the specific *ways* the ascent is understood. However, I have argued that this motif is nonetheless related to a rather common cosmological perception, and accordingly, I have stressed the underlying similarities in these texts.

NOTES TO CHAPTER THREE

1. On this question see the notes of the Philadelphia Seminar on Christian Origins, University of Pennsylvania, "Heavenly Ascent in Graeco-Roman Piety," 18 October, 1977 (mimeographed). The most complete survey with full bibliography is by Alan Segal, "Heavenly Ascent in Hellenistic Judaism, Early Christianity and their Environment," *ANRW* 2.23 (1980): 1333-94. Gerhardt Lohfink, *Die Himmelfahrt Jesu* (Munich: Kostel-Verlag, 1971), pp. 32-74 offers a survey of ascent materials with some attempt at classification. Most recently there is Mary Dean-Otting, *Heavenly Journeys: A Study of the Motif in Hellenistic Jewish Literature* (Frankfurt: P. Lang, 1984), which, unfortunately, offers little more than a mere catalogue of texts.

2. He provides a convenient summary of his thesis in *Greek Piety* (New York: W . W. Norton, 1969), pp. 92-185, based on his larger *Geschichte der griechischen Religion*, 2 vols. (Munich: Beck, 1967). Also see his masterly survey

article, "History of Greek Religion in the Hellenistic and Roman Age," *HTR* 36 (1934): 251-75, and his more specific treatments of cosmology and astral mysticism: "The New Conception of the Universe in Late Greek Paganism," *Eranos* 44 (1946): 20-27; "Die astrale Unsterblichkeit und der kosmische Mystik," *Numen* 1 (1954): 106-19.

3. See *Greek Piety*, pp. 96-103.

4. See Thorkild Jacobsen, "Mesopotamia," *Before Philosophy*, ed. J. A. Frankfort (Baltimore: Penguin Books, 1946), pp. 137·217. See also the *IDB*, s.v. "Cosmogony," by T. H. Gaster, which includes a pictorial sketch of the ancient Hebrew conception of the universe and further bibliography.

5. "Hellenistic Religions," *The New Encyclopedia Britannica: Macropaedia*, 15th ed., 8:750, italics mine. Also see Morton Smith, "The Common Theology of the Ancient Near East," *JBL* 71 (1952): 135-47.

6. For example, the picture of the underworld differs considerably in a text from the Hebrew Bible such as Job 3:11-19 from that of Odysseus' journey to Hades (Homer, *Odyssey* 11. 487-91) or from an Ancient Near Eastern text such as "Descent of Ishtar to the Nether World," (See *ANET*, pp. 106-8). Nonetheless, in all three one finds a fairly uniform evaluation of death and the underworld as a gloomy, undesirable, and irreversible state.

7. Cf. Isa. 27:1; 51:9-10; Psa. 89:9-12; Job 9:13-14; 26:12-13, not to mention Gen. 1:1-2:3. The pioneering study is Hermann Gunkel, *Schöpfung und Chaos in Urzeit und Endzeit* (Gottingen: Vandenhoeck & Ruprecht, 1895).

8. Quotations of the Hebrew Bible in this chapter are from the RSV unless otherwise noted, however, I have rendered the name LORD as Yahweh and at times added italics.

9. See Psa. 6:4-6; Isa. 38:9-20; Job 38:9-20; Job 3:11-19; 10:18-22. Of the many studies dealing with Hebrew concepts of death and afterlife I would mention the survey chapter by S. G. F. Brandon, *The Judgment of the Dead* (New York: Charles Scribner's Sons, 1967), pp. 56-75, which footnotes the more important literature. Alexander Heidel, (*The Gilgamesh Epic and Old Testament Parallels* [Chicago: University of Chicago Press, Phoenix Books, 1963], pp. 137-223) surveys the primary texts, cites important secondary literature, and discusses parallel ideas in Mesopotamian materials. However, Heidel's study is seriously flawed by his attempt to read hints of an idea of immortality or resurrection into Hebrew Bible texts.

10. R. H. Charles, *Eschatology: The Doctrine of a Future Life in Israel, Judaism and Christianity, A Critical History* (New York: Schocken Books, 1963, reprint of 1913 ed.), is still valuable, particularly for primary sources. More recently are the studies of W. E. Nickelsburg, Jr. (*Resurrection, Immortality, and Eternal Life in Intertestamental Judaism* [Cambridge: Harvard University

Press, 1972]) and H. C. C. Cavallin, (*Life After Death: Paul's Argument for the Resurrection of the Dead in I Cor. 15: Part I: An Enquiry into the Jewish Background* [Lund: GWK Gleerup, 1974]).

11. This text is translated in S. N. Kramer, *Sumerian Mythology* (Philadelphia: The American Philosophical Society, 1944), pp. 51-53, italics mine. See the suggested revisions of Thorkild Jacobsen in his review of Kramer's book, now conveniently published in *Toward the Image of Tammuz*, ed. William L. Moran (Cambridge: Harvard University Press, 1970), pp. 111-14.

12. On the well known Babylonian creation epic, *Enuma elish* see the text and notes in Pritchard, *ANET*, pp. 60-72, as well as Alexander Heidel, *The Babylonian Genesis* (Chicago: University of Chicago Press, Phoenix Books, 1963). For other texts which might be compared with this ancient Sumerian poem see the following materials in Pritchard, *ANET*: "The Worm and the Toothache," (pp. 100-101); "The Myth of Zu," (pp. 111-13); "Hymn to Amon-Re," (pp. 365-67).

13. The *Gilgamesh Epic* 10. 3, translation in Pritchard, *ANET*, p. 90, italics mine. For a survey of ancient Mesopotamian ideas of afterlife see Brandon, *Judgement of the Dead*, pp. 49-55 and Thorkild Jacobsen, *Before Philosophy*, pp. 217-34. I have mentioned previously Heidel, *Gilgamesh Epic*, pp. 137-223, which discusses Mesopotamian materials as well as Hebrew Bible texts.

14. The *Gilgamesh Epic* 7. 4. For other related texts see Pritchard, *ANET*: "Inanna's Descent to the Nether World," (pp. 52-56); "Descent of Ishtar to the Nether World," (pp. 106-8); "A Vision of the Nether World." (pp. 109-10).

15. A reconstruction of the details of Hesiod's cosmology is quite complicated. At the outset there is the problem of a reliable text. See the study of Maja E. Pellikann-Engel, *Hesiod and Parmenides: A New View on their Cosmologies and on Parmenides' Proem* (Amsterdam: Adolf M. Hakkert, 1974), which contains a discussion of the problem, covers relevant secondary material and attempts a pictorial representation.

16. Translation by Hugh G. Evelyn-White, *Hesiod*, LCL (Cambridge: Harvard University Press, 1936), pp. 86-89. I have left out line 118, which many scholars take to be spurious. On this point, and for a summary of the scholarly discussion on the meaning of *chaos* , see Pellikann-Engel, *Hesiod and Parmenides*, pp. 38-48. Some would interpret this term to refer to the region or gap between heaven and earth, separated to make a place for humankind.

17. Ibid., pp. 456-57. Note the rather striking thematic parallels with Psa. 104.

18.
Homer, *Odyssey* 11. 487-91, trans. A. T. Marray, LCL (Cambridge: Harvard

University Press, 1924), 1:421. The classic study of Greek views of immortality is Erwin Rohde, *Psyche: The Cult of Souls and Belief in Immortality Among the Greeks* 8th ed. (New York: Harcourt Brace, 1925). A more recent survey article by Werner Jaeger, "The Greek Ideas of Immortality," (Ingersoll Lecture for 1958) is now conveniently found in *Immortality and Resurrection: Death in the Western World, Two Conflicting Currents of Thought*, ed. Krister Stendahl (New York: Macmillan, 1965), pp. 97-114. The older study by Franz Cumont (*Afterlife in Roman Paganism*, [New Haven: Yale University Press, 1922]) deals more with the later period, but contains some important observations about earlier views. The secondary literature on this subject is vast. For bibliography there is *OCD*², s.v. "Afterlife," by Francis R. Walton.

19. For his summary see *Greek Piety*, pp. 96-185. For other descriptions see E. R. Dodds, *Pagan and Christian in an Age of Anxiety* (New York: W. W. Norton, 1965), pp. 1-36; André-Jean Festugière, *Personal Religion Among the Greeks* (Berkeley: University of California Press, 1960); and Jonathan Z. Smith, "Hellenistic Religions."

20. For a detailed drawing of a later full-blown gnostic system see Kurt Rudolf, *Gnosis: The Nature and History of Gnosticism* (New York: Harper and Row, 1983), pp. 68-69. There were, of course, many variations within this overall cosmology, see Walter Burkert, *Lore and Science in Ancient Pythagoreanism* (Cambridge: Harvard University Press, 1972), pp. 299-337. For the earlier period until Aristotle see D. R. Dicks, *Early Greek Astronomy to Aristotle* (Ithaca: Cornell University Press, 1970). The influence of astrological ideas during the period was pervasive, see A. D. Nock, "Sarcophagi and Symbolism," *AJA* 50 (1946): 140-70. Jews and early Christians shared this cosmology for the most part, the seven spheres were thought to be ruled by angelic powers or demons, see Hans Bietenhard, *Die himmlische Welt*.

21. "Hellenistic Religions," p. 749, italics mine.

22. Ibid., p. 749. For example, the idea of the underworld as the abode of the dead, although typical of archaic materials, is still found in texts from the Hellenistic (even into the imperial) period. See Phil. 2:10 for an example from Paul, or Apuleius, *Metamorphoses* 11. 5, for an even later example, in which Isis claims to rule the heavens as well as the subterranean regions of the dead. In other texts this "underworld" is transferred to the lower levels of the expanded seven heaven cosmos (e.g. Cicero, *Republic* 6. 26. 29) or it disappears altogether.

23. See Smith's collection of essays in *Map Is Not Territory* and the retrospective sketch of his work in the preface, pp. ix-xvi. Also his review article, "Native Cults in the Hellenistic Period," *HR* 11 (1971): 236-49, contains an important summary description on Hellenistic religions.

24. "Hellenistic Religions," pp. 750-51.

25. The *Republic* 6. 9-26. I have used here the translation by C. W. Keyes, Cicero, *De Re Publica, De Legibus*, LCL(Cambridge: Harvard University Press, 1928), for all quotations of this text, italics are mine throughout. On the text in general see Georg Luck, "Studia Divina in Vita Humana: On Cicero's 'Dream of Scipio' and its Place in Graeco-Roman Philosophy," *HTR* 49 (1956): 207-18.

26. This might refer to the preexistence of the soul in heaven and its subsequent fall or incarnation, a commonplace idea in many texts of the period. On the other hand, the reference to a "return" could mean that Scipio is visiting the heavenly realm in his dream, but can ascend there at death.

27. The translation and italics are mine throughout. I have used the critical Greek edition *Hermès Trismégiste*, ed. A. D. Nock, trans. A.-J. Festugière, 4 vols. (Paris: Société d'Édition Les Belles Lettres, 1946-1954), 1 (1946): 6-28. I have followed the section numbers in this edition in my English translation.

28. The text here is corrupt. See the Notes in Nock and Festugière, Ibid., pp. 22-23.

29. See the various eschatological myths with their astronomical motifs in Plato: *Republic* 613 E; *Phaedrus* 246 B; *Timaeus* 41 D. Examples of texts later than Plato would be: Pseudo-Aristotle *On the Cosmos*; Plutarch *The Face of the Moon; On the Delays of Divine Justice* 563 D, *On the Sign of Socrates* 590 B; the so-called "Mithras Liturgy," *PGM* IV 475-830. For a recent survey of such materials with full notes see Burkert, *Pythagoreanism*, pp. 364-66.

30. I will discuss these and other related texts further on in this chapter.

31. See *The Theology of Jewish Christianity* (Chicago: Henry Regnery, 1964), p. 179.

32. See Robert Grant, *Gnosticism and Early Christianity* (New York: Harper & Row, 1966), passim. See Daniélou's interesting study, "Les Traditions secrètes des Apôtres," *Eranos* 31 (1962): 199-215.

33. "On the Problem of the Religio-Historical Understanding of Apocalypticism,"*JTC* 6 (1969): 152. See also John J. Collins, "Cosmos and Salvation: Jewish Wisdom and Apocalyptic in the Hellenistic Age," *HR* 17 (1977): 121-42; his book, *The Apocalyptic Imagination* New York: Crossroad, 1984); and Jonathan Z. Smith, "Wisdom and Apocalyptic," *Religious Syncretism in Antiquity*, ed. Birger A. Pearson (Missoula: Scholars Press, 1975), pp. 131-56. On the similarities between Greek and Jewish eschatology see the helpful little study by T. Francis Glasson, *Greek Influence in Jewish Eschatology* (London: S. P. C. K., 1961).

34. See Jonathan Smith's review of *Le origini dello gnosticismo*, edited by Ugo

Bianchi, *Kairos* 10 (1968): 298-302.

35. See my study, "Resurrection and Immortality: Paul and Poimandres," *Christian Teaching: Studies in Honor of LeMoine G. Lewis,* ed. Everett Ferguson (Abilene: Abilene Christian University Press, 1981), pp. 72-91 in which I attempt just such a comparison.

36. See his *Pagan and Christian*, p. 37. Jaeger calls it a "radical transvaluation of reality . . . the greatest revolution in human thought that had ever occurred. . . .", "The Greek Ideas of Immortality," *Immortality and Resurrection*, ed. Stendahl, p. 112.

37. See Price, "Punished in Paradise," and Johann Maier, "Das Gefahrdungsmotiv bei der Himmelsreise in der Judischen Apokalyptik und 'Gnosis,'" *Kairos* 5 (1963): 18-40.

38. I have followed the translation in Pritchard, *ANET*, pp. 101-3.

39. See Jacobsen's arguments in *Image of Tammuz*, ed. William Moran, pp. 48-51.

40. Translation in Pritchard, *ANET*, pp. 114-118.

41. Ibid., p. 118.

42. The text and translation is from A. Leo Oppenheim, "The Interpretation of Dreams in the Ancient Near East," *APS* 46 (1956): 259. See pp. 267, 282, and 287 for related texts.

43. This emphasis should not be seen in absolute contrast to the idea of revelation. Even in Deuteronomy Moses does "go up" to receive the commandments, in contrast to the people who must remain below (Deut. 5:5, 27; cf. the more complicated traditions running through Exodus 19:16-25; 20:21; 24:1-18; 34:1-9). This type of ascent will be examined below.

44. Compare Sirach 34:1-8 on divinations, dreams and omens. Chapter 43 offers a summary of the type of piety Sirach espouses. It is possible that here in 3:21-22, as well as 43:31-32, we have specific protests against claims of ascent or the knowledge of heavenly lore; something highly valued among various Jewish groups from at least the 3rd century B.C.E. on.

45. See J. W. McKay, "Helel and the Dawn-Goddess: A Reexamination of the Myth in Isaiah 12-15," *VT* 20 (1970): 541-64. Compare Ezekiel 28:11-19, which appears to be related to a variant version of the Eden story (Gen. 3:22-24). The Ugaritic story of Attar, the god who tries to take Baal's seat, might serve as a parallel here. He sits on the throne but his feet do not reach the footstool and his head does not reach the top. He then concludes that he can not be a king in the heights of heaven and he descends. See P. C. Craigie,

"Helel, Athtar and Plaethon," *ZAW* 85 (1973): 223-25. Interest in this text, as an example of ascent as an invasion, continues well into our own era, e.g., see *Mekilta Shirah* chap. 6.

46. Whether or not Lucian is dependent on a source from Menippus, that he casts his tale in an archaic framework illustrates the point I noted earlier (following Jonathan Smith) about "persistence and change" being characteristic in this period.

47. I have used the translation of A. H. Harmon, *Lucian*, LCL, 8 vols. (Cambridge: Harvard University Press, 1915), 2: 268-323, italics are mine throughout.

48. See his *Pythagoreanism*, p. 359. Burkert rightly cautions against an overly static category of "Homeric religion," noting that a large number of overlapping and contradictory themes are present in the archaic period. He questions the thesis that the belief in an immortality among the stars was somehow forced upon the Greeks as a result of a developing and expanded science of astronomy from the time of Pythagoras on (pp. 356-60). I do not intend to suggest any kind of etiological argument in this regard, as if a cosmological revolution *caused* this fundamental shift away from the perception of the earth as the human place. Rather I am interested in how the idea of the heavenly journey is characteristically perceived during this period, *given* this cosmological development.

49. The Sumerian King List names one Enmenduranna, who like Enoch (Gen. 5:24) is the seventh of ten. The text is in Pritchard, *ANET*, pp. 265-66. This material is discussed by Thorkild Jacobsen, *The Sumerian King List* (Chicago: University of Chicago Press, 1939), pp. 74-75.

50. I have quoted the text from Geo Widengren, *The Ascension of the Apostle and the Heavenly Book* (Uppsala: A. B. Lundequistska, 1950), pp. 7-8.

51. Ibid., pp. 22-39.

52. Compare the units in Exodus 24:9-11, 12-15a, 15b-18a. For a literary analysis see Walter Beyerlin, *Origins and History of the Oldest Sinai Traditions* (Oxford: Blackwells, 1961). In later Jewish tradition Moses is called to heaven, e.g., *b. Shabbat* 88b; *Pesikta Rabbati* 20.

53. On later traditions of the enthronement of Moses see Wayne A. Meeks, "Moses as God and King," *Religions in Antiquity*, ed. Jacob Neusner, (Leiden: E. J. Brill, 1968), pp. 354-71, and his book, *The Prophet-King* (Lieden: E. J. Brill, 1967).

54. There are other visions of the enthroned deity in the Hebrew Bible, Exodus 24:9-11 I have just mentioned, also 1 Kings 22:19; Ezekiel 1 and 10; Dan. 7:9-10.

55. In general see Michael Stone, "Lists of Revealed Things in the Apocalyptic Literature," *Magnalia Dei* (Garden City: Doubleday, 1976), pp. 439-43.

56. I am using the translation of E. Isaac, in *OTP* 1: 13-89 for *I Enoch*, italics and [ ] are mine. The work as we presently have it seems to contain five sections which are variously dated, see Isaac's introduction and notes, 1: 5-12. *The Book of the Watchers* may be from the third century B.C.E., though attempts to date this material are problematic. About half of this section of the cycle is contained in Aramaic fragments from Cave 4 of Qumran. See J. T. Milik, *The Books of Enoch: Aramaic Fragments of Qumran Cave 4* (Oxford: Clarendon Press, 1976), pp. 22-41. For a summary discussion of the older material of the Enoch cycle see Michael Stone, *Scriptures, Sects and Visions* (Philadelphia: Fortress Press, 1976), pp. 27-56. There is an extensive bibliography on the Enoch materials in *The Pseudepigrapha in Modern Research With a Supplement*, James H. Charlesworth (Scholar's Press, 1981; reprint of the 1976 edition with a supplement), pp. 98-103, 278-283.

57. On the provenance of this material see Stone, *Scriptures, Sects and Visions*, pp. 34-35. One should compare here *The Astronomical Book* (chapters 72-82), which also seems to be one of the older sections of the Enoch cycle. There Enoch receives a revelation of astronomical and calendrical lore from the holy angel Uriel. He reports in the first person what he "saw," yet the explicit motif of ascent is lacking. These two sections of *1 Enoch* show that ascent and epiphany can have similar functions, both involve a reception of revelation in which the visionary experience lends authority to the content.

58. See the introduction, translation and notes of H. C. Kee, *OTP*, 1: 775-81; 788-95. There are some Aramaic fragments of this text from Qumran and elsewhere.

59. See the introduction, translation and notes by M. D. Johnson, *OTP*, 2: 249-95. The Greek text known as the *Apocalypse of Moses* parallels this Latin version in places. Johnson translates both side by side.

60. Compare *ApMos* 37-40. The chariot here seems to be the means of Adam's ascent and at the same time the throne upon which God sits.

61. See the introduction, translation and notes by R. Rubinkiewicz, with revised translation and notes by H. G. Hunt, *OTP*, 1: 681-705. The text is extant only in an Old Slavonic translation, perhaps of a Hebrew original.

62. This expansion into seven heavens is possibly due to a Slavic editor. The description of the first three is similar to the *TLevi* 3:1-4. See the notes of Rubinkiewicz and Hunt, *OTP*, 1: 698f.

63. Hermann Diels, ed., *Poetarum Philosophorum Fragmenta* (Berlin: Weidmann, 1901), pp. 48-73. On the text in general see Leonard Taran, ed.,

THINGS UNUTTERABLE: PAUL'S ASCENT TO PARADISE

Parmenides: A Text with Translation, Commentary and a Critical Essay (Princeton: Princeton University Press, 1965).

64. Frag. 1, lines 22-32, italics are mine.

65. On this message see the comments of A. H. Coxon in *OCD*[2], s.v. "Parmenides."

66. Pellikaan-Engel, *Hesiod and Parmenides*, pp. 63-78, surveys the positions of the major studies.

67. Of the many studies I would note as among the more important the following: Wilhelm Bousset, "Die Himmelsreise der Seele," *ARW* 4 (1901): 136-69, 229-73; Franz Cumont, "Le mysticism astral dans l'antiquite," *BARB* 58 (1909); 256-86, and his two books, *Astrology and Religion Among the Greeks and Romans* (New York: G. P. Putnam's Sons, 1912) and *Afterlife in Roman Paganism* (New Haven: Yale University Press, 1923); Rohde, *Psyche*; W. K. C. Guthrie, *The Greeks and their Gods* (Boston: Beacon Press, 1950); A. D. Nock, "The Cult of Heroes," *HTR* 37 (1944): 141-74; L. R. Farnell, *Greek Hero Cults and Ideas of Immortality* (Oxford: Clarendon Press, 1921); Richard Meyer, "Himmelfahrt," *RGG*[3] 3: 333-35; Martin Nilsson, "Die astrale Unsterblichkeit und der kosmische Mystik," *Numen* 1 (1954): 106-19; Carston Colpe, "Die Himmelsreise der Seele als philosophie-und religionsgeschichtliche Problem," *Festschrift für Joseph Klein*, ed. Erich Fries (Göttingen: Vandenhoeck & Ruprecht, 1967), pp. 85-104; Morton Smith, *Clement of Alexandria*, pp. 195-278; D. Roloff, *Gottähnlichkeit, Vergöttlichung und Erhöhung zu seligem Leben: Untersuchungen zur Herkunft der platonischen Angleichung an Gott* (Berlin: W. de Gruyter, 1970)

68. For example, on the debate between Origin and Celsus over Jesus' status, see Eugene Gallagher, *Divine Man or Magician?: Celsus and Origen on Jesus* (Missoula: Scholar's Press, 1982).

69. Guthrie, *The Greeks and their Gods*, p. 239.

70. David E. Aune lists these and others with examples and references in "The Problem of the Genre of the Gospels: A Critique of C. H. Talbert's What is a Gospel?," *Gospel Perspectives: Studies of History and Tradition in the Four Gospels* (Sheffield: JSOT, 1981), 1: 20-34.

71. The classic study on the "divine man" is Ludwig Bieler, *THEIOS ANER: Das Bild des "Göttlichen Menschen" in Spätantike und Frühchristentum*, 2 vols. (Vienna: Oskar Hofels, 1935-36; reprint ed. in one vol., Darmstadt: Wissenschaftliche Buchgesellschaft, 1976). For a history of research see Morton Smith, "Prolegomena to a Discussion of Aretologies, Divine Men, the Gospels and Jesus," *JBL* 90 (1971): 174-99 and more recently his article, "On the History of the Divine Man," *Paganisme, Judaïsme, Christianisme* (Paris: de Boccard, 1978), pp. 335-45. On ruler worship see Elias Bickermann, "Die

römische Kaiserapotheose," *ARW* 27 (1929): 1-27 and A. D. Nock, "Ruler-Worship and Syncretism," *Essays on Religion and the Ancient World* (Cambridge: Harvard University Press, 1972), 2: 551-558, and "Notes on Ruler-Cult I-IV," 1: 134-159.

72. Cumont, *Astrology and Religion*, p. 96; *Afterlife*, p. 95-96.

73. See Burkert, *Pythagoreanism*, pp. 357-68 and the studies on Greek ideas of immortality mentioned above, note 181.

74. Translation is mine. Hermann Diels, *Die Fragmente der Vorsokratiker*, ed. Walther Kranz, 10th ed., 3 vols. (Berlin: Wiedmann, 1960-61), 1: 15-18.

75. Burkert, *Pythagoreanism*, pp. 113, 259, 363 discusses the problem and cites the secondary literature.

76. In addition to the general studies already cited, see Richard Lattimore, *Themes in Greek and Latin Epitaphs* (Urbana: University of Illinois Press, 1942) and Franz Cumont, *Recherches sur le symbolisme funéraire des Romains*(Paris: P. Geuther, 19 42) along with Nock's review, "Sarcophagi and Symbolism," *Essays*, 2:606-41.

77. I have already mentioned Nickelsburg, *Resurrection*; Cavallin, *Life After Death;* Meeks, *Moses as God and King*.I would add here Carl Holladay, *Theios Anēr in Hellenistic Judaism* (Missoula: Scholar's Press, 1977).

78. Robert Grant called this point to my attention, see his treatment of the funeral scene in *Augustus to Constantine* (New York: Harper & Row, 1970), pp. 4-5.

79. "The Prayer of Joseph," *Map is Not Territory*, pp. 61-62. I have added "new" in [ ] based on further discussions with Smith of this thesis.

80. See Bruce Woll, "The Departure of the 'The Way,': First Farewell Discourse in the Gospel of John," *JBL* 99 (1980): 225-39.

81. Bousset was one of the first to emphasize this connection with final ascent. In his important survey article, "Die Himmelsreise der Seele," he states that the experience is "nichts anders als eine Anticipation der Himmelsreise der Seele nach dem Tode des Menschen." (p.136). Bousset's statement is too general. One has to take the evidence case by case.

82. On this text see James Adam, ed., *The Republic of Plato*, 2 vols. (Cambridge: University Press, 1929), 2: 433-63, 470-79.

83. See the introduction in Charles, *APOT*, 2: 163-80; Charlesworth, *OTP*, 1: 5-12; and the full-scale study of David W. Suter, *Tradition and Composition in the Parables of Enoch* (Missoula: Scholars Press, 1979). The dating of this part

of the Enoch cycle is most uncertain, perhaps before 70 C.E.

84. I have used the translation in Charles, *APOT*, 2:208-37, italics are mine throughout.

85. The enthronement of the "Elect One" in *1 Enoch* 61:6-13 seems to be based on 39:3-4. On this figure see Suter, *Tradition and Composition*, pp. 116-17.

86. On the composition of this section see Suter, Ibid., pp. 125-26.

87. Isaac takes the expression as merely an address ("You, son of man"), not a title (*OTP* 1: 50). For discussion see the comments of Suter, *Tradition and Composition*, pp. 12-13, 25, 27, 107, 170-75 and the bibliography in Charlesworth, *Pseudepigrapha*[supp], pp. 100-103, 278-283. Compare the dream of Moses in Ezekiel the Tragedian's *Exagoge* 668-82, where he is crowned and seated on God's throne and sees all the heavenly powers bow down before him (text in M. Denis, *Fragmenta pseudepigraphorum quae supersunt Graeca* [Leiden: E. J. Brill, 1970], pp. 210-160).

88. See the introduction, notes and translation by F. I. Anderson in *OTP* , 1: 91-213. I have cited the translation in Charles, *APOT*, 2:431-69.

89. I have used the translation in Hennecke-Schneemelcher, *NTA*, 2:642-66, italics are mine and I have dropped archaic pronouns and verbs. The entire work is preserved only in Ethiopic.

90. The classic study is Gershom Scholem, *Jewish Gnosticism*. More recently are the important studies of Ithamar Gruenwald, *Apocalpytic and Merkavah Mysticism* (Lieden: E. J. Brill, 1980) and David J. Halperin, *The Merkabah in Rabbinic Literature* (New Haven: American Oriental Society, 1980). Both of these discuss the more important secondary literature. Scholem provides a convenient list of the more important *Hekhalot* materials (*Jewish Gnosticism*, pp. 5-7). The most basic talmudic source is *b. Hagigah* 12

91. I have used an unpublished Hebrew text of Scholem and Wirszubski, graciously provided by Morton Smith. Smith is preparing a critical edition with translation and commentary. In general see his article, "Observations on Hekhalot Rabbati," *Biblical and Other Studies*, ed. A. Altmann (Cambridge: Harvard University Press, 1963), pp. 142-60. There is an English translation in David Blumenthal, ed., *Understanding Jewish Mysticism* (New York: KTAV, 1978), pp. 56-89. The best published Hebrew text is Solomon Wertheimer, ed., *Batte Midrashot*, 2 vols. (Jerusalem: Mossad Karav Kook, 1968), 1: 90-114. Gruenwald, *Apocalyptic and Merkavah Mysticism*, pp. 150-73, also discusses this text.

92. *Jewish Gnosticism*, p. 17-18. Morton Smith writes me that he sees no evidence in *Hekhalot Rabbati* that the initiate understood his ascent as having

anything to do with afterlife, or that he anticipated returning permanently to heaven.

93. See J. Gwyn Griffiths, *The Isis Book* (Leiden: E. J. Brill, 1975), which contains an introduction, translation, and detailed commentary. Griffiths gives a full biography of all important studies into the 1970's (pp. 362-87). Note as well the treatments of A. D. Nock, *Conversion: The Old and the New in Religion from Alexander the Great to Augustine of Hippo* (Oxford: University Press, 1961), pp. 138-55; A.-J. Festugiere, *Personal Religion Among the Greeks* (Berkeley: University of California Press, 1960), pp. 68-84; and Reitzenstein, *Hellenistic Mystery-Religions*, pp. 274-92. Nock calls book 11 "the high-water mark of the piety which grew out of the mystery religions" (p. 138).

94. I have used the Latin text and English translation of Griffiths, *The Isis-Book*, italics are mine throughout.

95. I quoted earlier the section in 11. 5 where Isis calls herself *regina manium*. A few lines down she says that the Siculi call her *Ortygiam Proserpinam*. Perhaps Isis and Proserpina are to be identified.

96. See the discussion and references to secondary literature in Griffiths, Ibid., 297-98.

97. Note Isis' claim to be *elementorum omnium domina* in the passage quoted above (11. 5). Col. 2:20 seems to offer a double parallel, "You have *died* with Christ, being freed from the *elemental spirits of the cosmos*." On baptism and the mystery religions see Günther Wagner, *Pauline Baptism and the Pagan Mysteries*.

98. See 11. 5 quoted above. This is the interpretation of Reitzenstein, *Hellenistische Wundererzählungen*, 2d. ed. (Stuttgart: B. G. Teubner, 1963), pp. 116-20.

99. See 11.21 where Lucius is told that to undergo the rite is like taking on a "voluntary death" and a recovery back to health.

100. I mentioned earlier the golden *lamella* found in ancient Mediterranean tombs. In some of those texts the initiate, though in the underworld, expects release to some kind of eternal life above (or perhaps "beyond").

101. The best critical Greek text, which I have followed, is Nock and Festugiere. Of the many studies of this tractate I would mention: Richard Reitzenstein, *Poimandres: Studien zur griechisch-ägyptischen und frühchristlichen Literatur* (reprint ed., Stuttgart: B. G. Teubner, 1966); André Festugière, *La revelation d'Hermès Trismégiste*, 4 vols. (Paris: Gabalda, 1944-54) and *Hermétisme et Mystique Paienne* Paris: Aubier-Montaigne, 1967); and C. H. Dodd, *The Bible and the Greeks* (London: Hodder & Stoughton, 1935).

THINGS UNUTTERABLE: PAUL'S ASCENT TO PARADISE

There is an English translation in *Documents for the Study of the Gospels*, ed. and trans. David R. Cartlidge and David L. Dungan (Philadelphia: Fortress Press, 1980), pp. 243-251. The older edition of Walter Scott and A. S. Ferguson (*Hermetica*, 4 vols. [Oxford: Clarendon Press, 1924-26]) suffers from Scott's drastic editing and speculative reconstructions.

102. The Greek text with a German translation is found in Karl Preisendanz,

Papyri Graecae Magicae, 2d. ed., edited by Albert Henrichs, 2 vols. (Stuttgart: B. G. Teubner, 1973-74), 1:88-101, cited here as *PGM*. Compare the recent edition edited by Hans Dieter Betz, *The Greek Magical Papyri in Translation*, vol. 1 (Chicago: University of Chicago Press, 1986). The classic study is by Albrecht Dieterich, *Eine Mithrasliturgie*, 3d ed., edited by Otto Weinreich (Leipzig: B. G. Teubner, 1923). I have used here the translation of Marvin W. Meyer, *The "Mithras Liturgy"* (Missoula: Scholars Press, 1976), italics are mine.

103. See Morton Smith's argument in "Transformation by Burial," *Eranos* 52 (1983), pp. 109-110.

104. "Heavenly Ascent," p. 1345.

105. For a survey of texts and a discussion of this question see D. S. Russell, *The Method and Message of Jewish Apocalyptic* (Philadelphia: Westminster Press, 1964), pp. 158-77. See also S. Niditch, "The Visionary," *Figures in Ancient Judaism* (Missoula: Scholars Press, 1980), pp. 153-79 and Michael Stone, "Apocalyptic--Vision or Hallucination," *Milla wa-Milla* 14 (1974): 47-56.

106. See the discussion of Gruenwald, *Merkavah Mysticism*, pp. 85-97. He concludes that some actual experience of ecstatic ascent must be *a priori* behind these materials, based on an analysis of the terminology used in the literary sources. See Jacob Neusner's analysis of the stories of this type which surround Yohanan ben Zakkai, "The Development of the *Merkavah* Tradition," *JSJ* 2 (1971): 149-60. Whether it can be maintained that the *merkabah* visionary material can be traced back to Yohanan's own life and thought or not, this kind of material did not develop from mere armchair speculation. Neusner's comment to this effect remains valid, see *A Life of Yohanan ben Zakkai* (Leiden: E. J. Brill, 1970), p. 137. See Halperin's review of the history of interpretation and his conclusions, *The Merkabah in Rabbinic Literature*, pp. 88-91, 117-20, 179-185.

107. See Walter Burkert, "GOES: Zum griechischen 'Schamanismus,' *RhM* 105 (1962): 36-55 and his discussion of texts in *Pythagoreanism*, pp. 120-65. I would also note the more general studies of E. R. Dodds, *The Greeks and the Irrational* (Berkeley: University of California Press, 1971) and Mircea Eliade, *Shamanism* (Princeton: Princeton University Press, 1974).

108. The setting of the vision in 1. 1 is quite specific, pointing to some trance state, although no details as to technique are given. For parallels see

the notes of Nock, *Hermes Trismegiste*, 1: 6-8. On visionary experience in general during this period see Nock's article, "A Vision of Mandulis Aion," *HTR* 27 (1934): 53-104.

109. See the reference to literary and archaeological materials related to Isiac initiation in Griffiths, *The Isis-Book*, pp. 286-308.

110. See his *Jewish Gnosticism*, pp. 14-19. Strictly speaking, by "gnosis" Scholem does not mean Gnosticism, the developed systems known to us from the Christian fathers. He has in mind esoteric lore about the heavenly world.

111. "The Angelic Liturgy at Qumrân--4Q Serek Širôt ʿÔlat Haššabbāt," *VTS* 7 (1960): 318-45.

112. This is the position of Gruenwald, *Merkavah Mysticism*, see his introduction, pp. vii-xi. See Halperin's reservations about including Tannaitic and Amoraic evidence in Scholem's long line of mystical tradition, *The Merkabah in Rabbinic Literature*, pp. 179-185.

113. See his chapter, "The Four Who Entered Paradise and Paul's Ascension to Paradise," in *Jewish Gnosticism*, pp. 14-19. Also there is the later study of John Bowker, "'Merkabah Visions' and the Visions of Paul," *JSS* 16 (1971): 157-73.

114. Especially see Daniélou's "Les Traditions secrètes des Apôtres" and Grant's "Early Alexandrian Christianity," *CH* 40 (1971): 133-44.

115. "Observations on Hekhalot Rabbati," pp. 159.

116. Ibid., p. 153-5.

CHAPTER 4

PAUL'S ASCENT TEXT

In this final chapter I shall examine Paul's ascent text in some detail and attempt to draw some conclusions in the light of the two previous chapters. What might this experience have involved and how was it significant for Paul?

The 2 Corinthians 12:2-4 Text

As I pointed out in chapter 2, most of the recent studies by New Testament scholars who have dealth with Paul's ascent account have focused on the identity of his opponents at Corinth and how he goes about defending his apostleship in that situation. Having already dealt with that broader issue, here I am interested in the account per se, which is sketched out in three short verses. What can it tell us about his experience? Paul writes:

> I know a man in Christ who fourteen years ago--whether in the body or out of the body I do not know, God knows--was caught up to the third heaven. And I know that this man--whether in the body or separate from the body I do not know, God knows-- was caught up into Paradise and he heard unutterable words which are unlawful to speak.

A simple reading of the text immediately suggests a number of obvious and basic questions:

1. Why does Paul use the third person here?

2. Is there any special significance to the dating of the revelation "fourteen years ago"?

3 Is Paul reporting a single experience, two separate experiences, or perhaps one experience but in two stages? Is Paradise equivalent to or located in "the third heaven" or is it something different?

4. Is there something at stake in whether the ascent was "in the body or out of the body," a phrase he repeats twice?

6. Why the emphasis on secrecy?

113

THINGS UNUTTERABLE: PAUL'S ASCENT TO PARADISE

These have been the focus of most of the exegetical treatments of the text and the basic evidence, though discussed over a period of decades, was essentially laid out by Windisch in 1924.[1] Before proceeding it will be helpful to set the two sections of the report in synoptic form. I will number the separate elements for convenient reference:

(a)	(b)
1. I know a man in Christ	1. And I know that this man
2. *fourteen years ago*	2.------------
3. whether in the body or out of the body I do not know	3. whether in the body or separate from the body I do not know
4. God knows	4. God knows
5. was caught up *to the third heaven*	5. *was caught up* into Paradise
6. - - - - - - - - -	6. *he heard words which are unlawful to speak*

One can immediately see that the account breaks into two quite parallel parts. The essential differences, which I have put in italics, are three: 1) part (a) speaks of the destination of the journey as "the third heaven," while (b) speaks of entering "Paradise"; 2) part (b) lacks the chronological note "fourteen years ago"; 3) part (a) lacks the concluding note about the result of the journey and its esoteric nature. I will now take up the basic questions I have listed above.

The Third Person and the Date

First, there is no question, despite the use of the third person, that Paul is reporting his own experience, that he is that "man in Christ." This is clear from 12:7-10, where he speaks of his temptation to be elated by this extraordinary revelation and the resulting harassment from Satan which the Lord allows to remind him of his place. As Betz has shown, Paul is following an apologetic literary tradition which makes us of ironic boasting.[2] Paul is taking no credit for this exalted experience, the visions and revelations are from the Lord (12:1, subjective genitive). He ironically boasts of "weakness" (v. 5), but the weakness he has in mind came as a *result* of this very privileged experience, namely the harassing angel of Satan (vv. 7-10).

The reference to the date seems to indicate how very important this experience was to Paul. It reminds one of his defense in Galatians where he gives precise dates for his conversion and his visits to Jerusalem (Gal. 1:15-2:1). When it comes to such a landmark experience he has the exact date well in mind.[3] If this section of the letter was written in the early 50's C.E., then the ascent took place around the year 40, during the formative years of his ministry, perhaps in the area of Syria-Cilicia. Attempts to correlate this experience with his conversion or any other event we know in his life seem impossible.[4] This precise dating by Paul might have something to do also with the issue of authenticity. His testimony is concrete and specific, as he says in 12:7, he is "speaking the truth." In any case, the experience is vividly remembered and obviously important to Paul, even after more than a decade.

A Two-Stage Journey?

Most interpreters would agree that despite the parallel form of Paul's report, we are most likely dealing with a single experience. It is precisely dated and the elements which are repeated are parallel to the point of redundancy. So why does Paul repeat himself, using almost the same words, if he is speaking of one journey to heaven? As I have noted, other than the introductory chronological note and the concluding note about secrecy, the only significant difference in the two parts is the reference to destination--to the third heaven or into Paradise (my # 5 above). It is here we must focus our attention. Either the "third heaven" and "Paradise" are the same destination, or they are different. If they are the same, then this parallel style is truly redundant. Paul says the same thing two times using the same language almost word for word. If these refer to different destinations, then we would have a single journey reported in two stages, i.e., he was taken up to the third heaven, and then to Paradise. This would parallel the way Lucian reports Menippis' flight to heaven to see Zeus, first to the moon, then on up to the highest heaven (*Icaromenippus* 22). I think this parallel structure supports the idea of a two-stage journey. But what about the specific language used here for both the journey and its destination/s?

Paul uses the verb translated here "caught up" (*harpazō*) one other time, in 1 Thess. 4:17, where he is explaining how the dead and living will be taken up to meet Jesus in the air when he returns (this prophetic information came to him by revelation, a "word of the Lord" he says--v. 15). Some have argued on the basis of this verb that Paul's ascent was "involuntary." Lincoln, while not entirely ruling out the possibility of "preparations," comments:

> It would seem to indicate that Paul's experience was an involuntary one where God took the initiative rather than one brought about by preparation or special techniques (cf. other uses of *harpazo* in the sense of "to catch up" where God or his Spirit are clearly those who perform the act--Wisd. iv.11; Acts viii.39; 1 Thess. iv. 17; Rev. xii. 5).[5]

THINGS UNUTTERABLE: PAUL'S ASCENT TO PARADISE

This is to misunderstand the nature of visionary experience as something *granted* by a deity. The idea of one being empowered to "ascend to heaven" or that one is "caught up" or "borne aloft" in no way precludes special preparation or techniques. Conversely, for one to employ special preparation or techniques in no way implies that a visionary experience is somehow self-achieved. This misunderstanding is related to the idea that magic is compelling the deity and involves spells, amulets, or paraphernalia, while religion has to do with devotion, and is somehow a purer activity.[6] For example, in the "Mithras Liturgy" there are various special preparations and magical techniques connected with the ascent, however the experience is one graciously granted by the deity. The opening ritual begins:

> Draw in breath from the rays, drawing up three times as much as you can, and you will see yourself *being lifted up* and ascending to the height, so that you seem to be in mid-air (lines 538-41, italics mine).

Throughout the text the initiate must rely upon heavenly guides or deities (lines 630-34) and must be *allowed* an audience before the supreme god (lines 640-44). The same is true in Apuleius' account of the Isis initiation. Throughout the account it is emphasized that Lucius must wait for the graceful call of the goddess. When the day of his initiation comes he has made special preparations for the experience (11. 22-23), but what takes place is granted through the power of the goddess. Indeed, I would take the phrase "I was carried through all the elements," in Apuleius' description of his experience was one of the best verbal parallels to Paul's use of *harpazō* in 2 Cor. 12:2-4. Whether it is likely that Paul underwent special preparations, took along amulets, or memorized secret spells in order to make this journey remains a speculative matter. But the use of this verb does not preclude such, it simply means he was *transported* up.

What can be said about his references to "the third heaven" and "Paradise"? Scholars have tried, without much success, to precisely identify his language in Jewish texts from this period which mention a plurality of heavens and locate Paradise. The evidence is quite complicated and contradictory. Various texts number the heavens differently: *3 Baruch* has five; *Testament of Levi* either three or seven, depending on the version; *Apocalypse of Abraham* and *Ascension of Isaiah* have seven. Seven heavens are named in *b. Hagigah* 12b and this numbering shows up in other scattered references in Tannaitic texts.[7] In non-Jewish texts, as I pointed out in chapter 3, we often encounter the notion of seven heavens, each seen as a planetary sphere. The *Apocalypse of Moses* refers twice to Paradise as located in the third heaven (37:5; 40:1), which at first glance might seem to offer the best parallel to Paul's reference. The text tells how Adam was taken there to be buried, so it appears to be the place of repose for the righteous until the end. It is unclear in this text whether other levels exist above the third. But there is another quite different reference to Paradise in 13:4. There it refers to a time after the resurrection of the dead, when all the righteous will dwell with God forever. Also, the Latin version of this text, the *Life of Adam and Eve*, which I mentioned in the previous chapter, uses the term in yet a third way. There Adam ascends before his death "into the Paradise of righteousness," but the reference is clearly to the highest heaven, the throne of God (25:3). So here we have three very different meanings given to the term Paradise within the same textual tradition. *2 Enoch* also seems to locate Paradise in the third heaven. Enoch moves up through the seven heavens to the throne of God, but on the way, at the third, he is shown Paradise, a place like the garden of Eden, prepared for the righteous as an eternal inheritance (8:1-9:1 [A,B], cf. 42:3 [A]). Yet later in the text, the term Paradise is used again, but this time to refer to the time after the judgment when all the righteous will dwell with God forever (65:10 [A,B]). Most of the references seem to fall into one of these two categories. Sometimes Paradise is used to describe the place of repose for the righteous dead (variously located); other times it is used to describe a final state at the end, a kind of new Edenic existence with God forever.[8] For example, in the *Apocalypse of Abraham* the patriarch is taken to the highest or seventh heaven, there he looks down and sees Paradise below, where the righteous dead dwell (21:6). The *Testament of Abraham* tells how he was taken to Paradise at the time of his death, to join the other righteous ones (20:14 [A]). In another version he is shown Paradise, where Enoch and others dwell, and is shown the judgment that goes on there (10:2-11:10 [B]). *1 Enoch* 60:8 and 61:12 seem to refer also to this dwelling place of the righteous. In contrast, *Testament of Levi* 18:10-14 and *Testament of Dan* 5:12 use Paradise to refer to the final Edenic state, the new Jerusalem at the end. This usage shows up a number of times in *4 Ezra* as well (7:36, 123; 8:52), where Paradise seems to represent eternal life in contrast to Hell. The only two references (besides this one by Paul) to Paradise in the New Testament reflect this identical double usage. In Luke 23:43, where Jesus tells the criminal on the cross, "Today you will be with me in Paradise," it seems to refer to a blessed place for the departed righteous, probably located in the lower Hadean world.[9] The other reference is Rev. 2:7, where it refers to a state of blessedness before the throne of God, upon a restored Edenic earth (Rev. 3:7; 22:1-5). Despite this diversity there is an underlying unity in this material. Paradise is an image rooted in Genesis 2-3, and refers to either a preserved or restored garden of Eden, a place or state of pleasantness, removed from sin, suffering, and death. Whether it is located above or below, in the present or in the future (and we have examples of all of these variations), it seems to always symbolize God's intimate presence and access to the tree of life. Other scholars have suggested that our best parallel is the story now preserved in Tannaitic sources about the four Rabbis who "entered Paradise (*pardes*)" (*T. Hagigah* 2:3-4; *p. Hagigah* 77b; *b. Hagigah* 14b, 15a,b).[10] Ben Azzai looked and died, Ben Zoma looked and was smitten, Aher (Elisha ben Abuyah) "cut the shoots," and Akiba "ascended safely and descended safely" (or "entered safely and went out"). They would take this reference to "Paradise" literally, as the goal of a mystical ascent or journey to heaven, the vision of the *merkabah*. Others have argued that Paradise in this tradition was originally metaphorical (meaning some type of wisdom or gnosis), and only later interpreted as a literal mystical ascent.[11]   Whether these texts provide evidence that these early Palestinian rabbis were involved in mystical experiences of ascent to heaven or not, the story itself, does seem to offer a strong parallel to Paul's language here about going up and "entering Paradise." His opponents at Corinth were Jews, and they were boasting over such experiences.   They seem to share a common world with Paul, who uses this technical language and expects to be understood. It seems likely that Scholem was correct; they were drawing upon the same mystical tradition that later shows up here and there in the Tannaitic texts.   Despite the historical distance, one has the sense that in both texts (especially in the BT version, along with the collection of traditions now in *b. Hagigah* 11b-16a) we are dealing with something quite similar.   Both seem to use the phrase "entering Paradise" as a technical term.   The strong implication in the BT version is that this means the highest heaven, it is no lower level achievement, only the holy Akiba enters and exits successfully.   It is connected with a vision of the *merkabah* throne of God.   I think the passage which offers us our best parallel for both Paul and these later Rabbis is in the *Life of Adam and Eve*, where Adam is taken up to heaven:

> I was carried off *into the Paradise* of righteousness, and *I saw the Lord sitting* and his appearance was unbearable flaming fire. And many thousands of angels were at the right and the left of the chariot (25:3)

This is a key text because it connects Paradise with the highest heaven, obviously using the term in a technical way, and reflects an interest in the *merkabah* or "chariot" throne of God.   It seems to offer us the best clue to Paul's language.   It also connects well with the later Rabbinic materials, which in turn seem to echo the way Paul used the term.

Since Paul uses the term "Paradise" in this very specific way, we can be fairly sure that he is drawing his vocabulary from this world of Jewish apocalyptic-mystical thought.   So what can one conclude from these texts? Since he speaks of going up to the third heaven, and *entering* Paradise, it seems we can eliminate the possibility that the term refers to a future time of blessedness for the righteous after the coming of Jesus and resurrection of the dead.   He does seem to locate it in his cosmos, and he says he went there and returned.   There are at least three main possibilities:

1. Paradise=the abode of the righteous dead=third heaven. I think this connection is the most unlikely. It is hard to imagine Paul *boasting* that he, like a legendary Enoch, has been shown the dwelling place of the dead.   For apocalyptic literary productions this is fine, but Paul's text comes out of his own world of visionary experience.   It is unlikely that archaic texts like *1 Enoch*, in which such touring is so vital, are of much interest to him, to say nothing of his opponents.   Given some of his other claims, his exalted sense of apostolic mission, and his expectation of the imminent overthrow of the

cosmos, such a claim would be almost laughable. Even in *2 Enoch*, seeing the place of the dead is merely a "tour stop" along the way, of little significance compared to entering the seventh heaven and beholding God's throne. Besides, Paul apparently does not think the dead are in heaven. The picture he presents in 1 Thess. 4:13-18 is that Jesus will *bring them forth* from the dead (this is the proper meaning of *axei* in v. 14, despite many English translations), that is, they will be awakened from their "sleep" and *rise* to meet Christ in the clouds, in the air. Paul is quite literal about this. He does expect that they will emerge from their tombs with new immortal bodies, but nonetheless, they still *rise* to heaven, they don't descend from heaven. Paul holds an idea that might be called "transformation by burial," and for him, *the body and its burial*, whether of Christ or the saints, is vital (1 Cor. 15)[12]

2. Paradise=throne of God=third heaven. This possibility would see Paradise as the highest level, the place where God dwells, but in a system of three heavens. Paul would then be speaking of a one-stage journey to the third heaven, and an entry into Paradise. That Paradise for Paul means the highest level, the throne of God, I think is also likely. He is not mentioning some second rate experience here. But it seems strange that he would *refer to the third heaven*, if he thought it was the highest. His report becomes redundant. To mention the third heaven is to hint at other levels beyond.

3. Paradise=throne of God=highest heaven (7th?). This seems to be the best interpretation. It satisfies more of the difficulties. Paradise is the goal of the journey, and it is the highest goal one could claim, something one could call "extraordinary," and over which one could easily become elated (2 Cor. 12:7). He reports it as a two stage journey, which accounts for the parallel structure. He has been to the third heaven, yes, but beyond that, he has entered Paradise. And it is there, in Paradise, before God's throne, that he hears things unutterable. This interpretation seems to best fit the structure and content of the report.

The language Paul uses for the heavenly world indicates that his cosmos is a vast one, populated with multiple levels of angelic beings. In Rom. 8:38-39 he mentions *aggeloi, archai, dunameis, hupsoma,* and *bathos*--which seem to be various powers below the level of God's throne (v. 34), all subjugated through the power of Christ.[13] He predicts the victory of Christ, in 1 Cor. 15:24, over "all rule, authority and power"(*archē, exousian, dunamin*)--all technical terms for the the various orders of heavenly rule. His references to the "elemental spirits of the cosmos" (*stoicheia tou kosmou*) point to some idea of ruling spirits, likely connected to the planetary spheres, who exercise power at various levels (Gal. 4:1-11, cf. Col. 2:8, 20).[14] This phrase, along with his numeration " *third* heaven" in the ascent passage, is the best evidence that his cosmos was divided into seven levels, corresponding to the seven planetary spheres. He refers in 1 Cor. 2:6 to these "rulers of the age" over whom he identifies Satan as head or "god" (2 Cor. 2:4; 1 Cor. 10:20; 121-3), and sees their reign as passing and doomed (1 Cor. 7:31; Gal. 1:4). Satan is able to blind unbelievers, destroy apostates, tempt believers sexually and otherwise, appear as a transformed angel of light, send deceiving angels, support his own apostles, preach a false gospel and dispense a counterfeit "holy spirit," and hinder and harass Paul (2 Cor. 4:4; 1 Cor. 5:5; 2 Cor. 2:11; 1 Cor. 7:5; 2 Cor. 11:14; Gal. 1:18; 2 Cor. 11:4, 13; 1 Thess. 2:18; 2 Cor. 12:7). The spiritual battles of which Paul speaks involve powerful heavenly forces able to destroy and even kill (1 Cor. 5:5; 10:30; 2 Cor. 11:1-6). The victory he expects is a cosmic one, over all these heavenly realms (1 Cor. 6:2-3). All of these references indicate a highly complex and dangerous cosmos with multiple levels.

We have every reason to believe that Paul's opponents at Corinth, those he labels "false apostles" and "deceitful" workers of Satan (2 Cor. 11:13-14) were putting forth their own claims to "visions and revelations" (2 Cor. 12:1). This was likely part of their claim to be superior (2 Cor. 11:5). We know they were Jews as well. Their claims might have included a variety of experiences related to communicating with the heavenly world, whether oracles, epiphanies or ascent to various levels of heaven, and as a result they likely claimed special *gnosis* in these esoteric areas. I would suggest that the way in which Paul relates his *two-stage journey* might be designed to counter such claims. First, he says that he *too* has had such revelations of heavenly secrets, even at the third level of heaven. I take it that this might have been an impressive claim in such a context, where various experiences were being compared (note 2 Cor. 10:12). Perhaps this very reference to "the third heaven" is a term he picked up from them, and had a very specific meaning to this group. It reminds one of the Tannaitic texts which speak of Rabbi Yohanan ben Zakkai and his circle being promised by a heavenly voice that they were designated for "the third set," which apparently means a level of achievement in the world beyond connected with knowledge of the secrets of the *merkabah* (b. *Hagigah 14b* and parallels).[15] Regardless, at this point Paul is willing to allow the opponents to identity their own claims with his. Then, with the second section of his account, he suddenly *distances* himself from their level of operations. Yes, he can relate visions and revelations; yes, he too has been as far as the third heaven; but he, moreover, has been taken *into* Paradise--he has appeared before God's very throne in the highest heaven. There he too heard words, but of such a nature that they cannot even be communicated to lower grade initiates. In this sense, I would agree with Betz regarding the irony of Paul's "revelation" which he is not to communicate. The situation Paul faced might well be like the one reflected in Colossians. The author warns against outsiders who claim visions:

> Let no one disqualify you, requiring various kinds of self-abasement and reverence for angels, relying upon things seen in visions of the heavenly world, puffed up without reason from a sensuous mind . . . (2:18).[16]

This lower level interest in the heavenly world is then contrasted with the "things above, where Christ is seated at the right hand of God" (3:1). The group is assured that when Christ returns, they will share with him the highest glory (3:4). The point is that such opponents were involved with "things below," with revelations received from the "principalities and powers" (2:15), the "elemental spirits of the cosmos" (2:20), who control the lower spheres of heaven. In the Colossian letter, which reflects a later stage of interpretation of Paul's thought, "looking above" to the "Head" comes to mean following the directives of the author. But in 2 Corinthians 10-12, it is Paul who embodies this very level of authority. He has personally been before the throne of God and received "things unutterable." Dealing with the heavenly world can be both dangerous and deceptive. Who is to distinguish the *aggeloi* of God from those of Satan? Paul's claim to have entered Paradise is a claim to have been approved by God, but ironically, its demonstration is the weakness that resulted--his "thorn in the flesh," the harassment he must constantly face. We must assume that Paul's references to both the third heaven and to Paradise would have technical meanings to his opponents. By making such a claim, with its ironic result of weakness, he makes his "boast," intending to completely separate himself from their level of operation. I do not mean that Paul's claim is a simple matter of one-upmanship. He is not just claiming a higher vision. He does not even recognize the opponents as being "in Christ" so his boast as a "man in Christ" of having entered Paradise is not to be classed with theirs. Still, it *is* an highly privileged and exalted revelation, the most one could claim, and it *is* authentically from the Lord (12:1, 7). Those aspects together serve to remove him from their arena of comparison.

In Or Out of the Body?

This twice repeated disavowal (vv. 2b, 3b) has often been seen as some kind of carefully designed statement in the light of the views his opponents and perhaps their followers in the Corinthian church.[17] It could well be that some were claiming their experiences were "out of the body" and making some point about that. Paul was certainly familiar with the notion of bodily translation, if only from the Hebrew Bible accounts of Enoch or Elijah, and he doubtless knew of claims of heavenly travel where one left the body.[18] This is not, as many seem to think, a "Jewish vs. Hellenistic" issue. Stories of bodily assumptions and travel of the "soul" outside the body are widespread and international. In so many of the texts which report some kind of ascent, it is simply unclear whether the journey was thought to be in or out of the body. I think we must take Paul's statement at face value. This journey to Paradise was something he experienced. His account is a testimony or witness to that. One might well ask, *how* did this happen? Were you actually taken up bodily or did your soul somehow leave your body and return? These are obvious questions that would be put to such a claim. His answer is that he simply does not know, the journey was something granted by the Lord, so only God could answer that type of question. He wants to separate what he knows--that he was taken into Paradise and received secret revelation--from what he does not know, just how this took place. The statement is mildly apologetic, and an indication of the genuineness of the account. This is precisely what one would expect to find in this type of first person claim.

Things Which Cannot Be Told

Paul says that in Paradise he heard "unutterable words which are unlawful to speak" (v. 4b). The term "unutterable words" (*arrēta hpēmata*) basically means "inexpressible."[19] In some texts it refers to something that cannot be expressed, something beyond human powers. Thus, a text from the Greek magical papyri explains it: "it is not able to be spoken by a human mouth" (*PGM* 13. 763, cf. *Poimandres* 31). It can mean something too sacred to express, something which is prohibited. Philo speaks of men biting off their tongues to avoid disclosing "*ta arrēta*"[20] It is possible that Paul had both meanings in mind, but more likely that he is emphasizing the first, since he follows it with the clear reference to secrecy and prohibition--"which are unlawful to speak." It is a word drawn from the vocabulary of the mystery cults and reflects the common motif of secrecy found in most Hellenistic religions.[21] One can compare the phrases *quae voce meliora sunt* and *dicerem, si dicere liceret*, connected with Lucius' Isis initiation (*Metamorphoses* 11. 23). Paul means that he has heard things far beyond the human realm. One should compare here the difficult passage in 1 Cor. 2:6-16. He speaks there of "*teleioi*" (v. 6) who can understand heavenly mysteries, even beyond the understanding of the lower angelic orders (v. 8). The Spirit has revealed things beyond human powers, what he calls "the deep things of God" (vv. 9-10). To have the Spirit is to actually share the *nous* of Christ (v. 16). We must assume that Paul is picking up on the technical language of his opponents here, the "spirituals," who must have made claims to heavenly secrets.[22] But, he applies these capacities to the community as a whole, to all who possess the Spirit. In view of this, what Paul claims to have received in Paradise was an even higher and more privileged revelation. It was *neither shared by, nor to be shared with*, others who possessed the Spirit.

The Significance of Paul's Ascent

Assuming that entering Paradise *does* mean that Paul was taken up to the highest heaven and given some extraordinary secret revelation, what significance might such an experience have had for him? Here I want to move a bit beyond the context of the report in 2 Corinthians 10-13. Given what he says in the report itself, what we know generally of the phenomenon of the heavenly journey in this period, and what appears to be his understanding of his unique mission and revealed message--what more can be said about the experience?

Paul does not emphasize what he *saw*, but what he *heard*. Unfortunately, unlike Apuleius, he will not even offer the Corinthians (or the later readers) even a small hint. We can only conclude that since it was something beyond human ability to utter and was to be kept secret, that he would have understood it to be a highly privileged revelation. But he does tell us what he *did*, namely he *entered* Paradise--that is, he was taken into the highest level of heaven, before God's throne. We might speculate a bit about this, though there is not a lot one can say, given the limited nature of his letters on this kind of subject. He does believe that Jesus has ascended to heaven, and has been given a place of rule at the right hand of God the Father (Phil. 2:10; 1 Cor. 15:24-28; Rom. 8:34). This is quite literal to him, for he speaks of him "descending from heaven," to the level of the clouds, and gathering his saints to join him in the air above the earth (1 Thess. 4:16-17). He has a glorious (shining?) body (Phil. 3:20-21). We can assume, that as an educated Jewish scholar, Paul would have pictured the throne of God in the highest heaven much like it is pictured in the Hebrew Bible (especially Exodus 24:9-11; Isaiah 6:1-5; and Ezekiel 1 and 10). We have no way of knowing to what extent he might have delved into any form of further speculation, akin to the *merkabah* lore, about the heavens and the throne of God, though it is hard to imagine that this would have been absent from his training as a scholar and teacher. We do know that since he uses technical terms for various levels of heavens and orders of angelic/demonic powers, none of which are found in the Torah or Prophets, and that in a general way he participates in this "explosion" of interest in the unseen world among Jews in Second Temple times. The main features of his apocalyptic vision are known to us from texts of the period, though as a prophet himself, he adds his own detailed revelations (such as 1 Thess. 4:16-17). So we can safely assume, that if entering Paradise meant being taken before God's throne, given Paul's beliefs and expectations, this would have been an absolutely extraordinary experience. In his world of men and angels, what could be greater than this ascent to heaven?

The only thing greater would be the events he expects to take place at the coming of Jesus *from* heaven. But there is a relationship between these two journeys, his and Jesus'. He expects two main things at Jesus' return. First that he (and the others) will be transformed from a mortal to a glorious immortal body, and second, that they will all "be with the Lord." He closes his apocalyptic section in 1 Thess. 4:13-18 by saying "and so we shall always be *with the Lord*." He tells them later in the letter that it doesn't matter if they die before the end, because either way they will "live together *with him*." When late in his career he thinks he might die before the end comes, he speaks of "departing to *be with Christ*," which I take as an indication that he expects by this time some special resurrection and ascent to heaven of his own (Phil. 1:23; 3:10-11). In such case, this would be a *return* to heaven for him, since he had already had this experience in the 40's C.E. In other words, there is a sense in which he has already, however briefly, "been with the Lord." What about his other expectation--the change of the decaying body? Obviously he does not think *his* body was changed on his journey to heaven. He knows he is flesh and blood and will die, and he expects that he might be resurrected like Christ (Phil.3:11). But if he has been in the highest heaven, and seen Christ "seated at the right hand" of God, in his shining immortal form, then he has actually already seen what is to come. In this sense his journey is proleptic and functions like some of the others I surveyed, as an anticipation or foretaste of what he expects to come. I would argue then, that his ascent to Paradise has the several direct connections with his message. If the core of that message has to do with glorification and rule with Christ at his coming, Paul's ascent reflects it completely. It is not mere theological speculation for him. He has been with Christ, he has experienced the glory and power he associates with Jesus, the very one who has been transformed from a mortal to an immortal son of God and who reigns over the whole cosmos at the right hand of God. Paul himself equates the power to rule with the power to transform (Phil. 3:22), so there is a direct connection between the two.

What about his mission? Given the perceptions he has of his special calling--that he was chosen before birth like a great prophet, that he has seen the Lord, that his mission to the Gentiles is a fulfillment of Isaiah's vision of the end and will bring about the final redemption of Israel, and (possibly) that he too, like Jesus, will die, be resurrected, and ascend to heaven before the end--this extraordinary experience of having already gone up once and received secret revelation only completes a picture. Next to his initial calling and conversion, (which is always unparalleled as a demonstration of God's overflowing grace in choosing one so unworthy for so great a task) his ascent to heaven must have been his highest moment. He says as much in 2 Cor. 12:7. Because he might be too elated over what he has been given, he is harassed for years by an angel of Satan so that he will always remember the lesson that suffering and weakness lead, paradoxically, to power and glory. He has had a taste of that power and glory, a special taste. This gives powerful conviction to all his statements about "beholding the glory of the Lord" (2 Cor. 3:18) or the slight momentary affliction which is to result in "glory beyond all comparison" (2 Cor. 4:17) or the sufferings of the present being unworthy of comparison with the "glory soon to be revealed" (Rom. 8:18).

Beyond this there is little one can say. I think the texts I examined in the previous chapter can shed light on Paul's experience. Broadly speaking he presents a Hellenistic way of salvation--a particular scheme of apotheosis, or "immortalization," with certain apocalyptic peculiarities. The broad contours of his religious experiences--epiphany, the reception of oracles, visions, the journey to heaven, secret revelations--these are all well known to us, especially from the Greek magical papyri, the Hermetic texts and various forms of esoteric Judaism of the period. Add to that his specific expectations regarding his mission to the Gentiles, the conversion of Israel, and the imminent *parousia* of Jesus as cosmic Lord, and you have it--his own particular vision and version of that most general Hellenistic (and human) hope- -*escape from mortality.* And yet it is those very apocalyptic "particulars" that make Paul really Paul. His was not a scheme of salvation for any place or for all time. Although he has endured and been appropriated in many different ways over the centuries, from the standpoint of the history of Judaism, he belongs in those crucial years of hope and promise, before the terrible days of August, 70 C.E., when many such dreams came to an end. For Paul the "appointed time" of the End had drawn *very near* (1 Cor. 7:26, 29, 31). How near, it is difficult to say, but he wrote that in the early 50's C.E.. If he, like others in the movement before 70 C.E., expected the fulfillment of Daniel 11 and 12, with the "desolating sacrilege" set up in the Temple at Jerusalem, then events such as Gaius' attempt to have his statue placed there (41 C.E.) would have fueled his apocalyptic speculations.[23] Apparently his plans to go to Spain never worked out, due to his arrest under Nero (Rom. 15:28), so his grand hope of bringing the bulk of Israel to accept Jesus as Messiah through his Gentile mission became more and more hopeless. By 70 C.E. it was becoming increasingly difficult to maintain any immediate hope for the "redemption of Israel."[24] Others could pick up the pieces in various ways, as Jacob Neusner and his students have demonstrated so clearly, but Paul was gone and what emerged in his name, even in the short decades after 70 C.E., was the beginning of a new and very different story.[25]

NOTES TO CHAPTER FOUR

1. The treatment of Windisch, *Der Zweite Korintherbrief*, pp. 366-80, remains the best. Lietzmann, *An die Korinther*, pp. 152-55, and Plummer, *Second Corinthians*, pp. 336-45, offer a fairly extensive discussion of the text. Reitzenstein has some helpful exegetical comments in his *Hellenistic Mystery-Religions*, pp. 469-85. The main recent studies are Betz, *Paulus und sokratische Tradition*, pp. 84-92; Barrett, *Second Corinthians*, pp. 305-18; Saake, "Paulus als Ekstatiker"; Spittler, "The Limits of Ecstasy"; Lincoln, "Paul the Visionary" and Baird, "Visions, Revelations, and Ministry."

2. *Paulus und sokratische Tradition*, pp. 89-100. On this "Bescheidenheitsstil" see Windisch, *Der Zweite Korintherbrief*, pp. 370-80. Note the rabbinic examples of third person references listed in *Str-B*, 3: 530-31.

3. Against Barrett, who sees it as an indication that Paul disparaged the experience and has to go back fourteen years for a suitable example! (*Second Corinthians*, p. 308).

4. See the recent treatments of Robert Jewett, *A Chronology of Paul's Life* (Philadelphia: Fortress Press, 1979), pp. 54-55; and Gerd Luedemann, *Paul Apostle to the Gentiles: Studies in Chronology* (Philadelphia: Fortress Press, 1984), who agree. John Knox argued at one point that the Paradise ascent was to be identified with his conversion, but he subsequently gave this up, see *Chapters in a Life of Paul* Nashville: Abingdon Press, 1950), pp. 77-78.

Morton Enslin and others have continued to maintain this possibility, see *Reapproaching Paul* (Philadelphia: Westminster Press, 1972), pp. 53-55. The main problems are that the reference to the Jerusalem meeting in Gal. 2:1 which would have to be dated 14 years before the conversion (see Gal. 1:18, "after three years")' with the meeting itself taking place in the same year as Paul writes this section of 2 Corinthians. Both seem unlikely.

5. "Paul the Visionary," p. 215

6. On this point see the helpful discussion of Morton Smith, *Clement of Alexandria*, pp. 220-222.

7. See the references in *Str-B*, 3: 531-32. In general the older but still useful discussion of Charles, *The Book of the Secrets of Enoch* (Oxford: Clarendon Press, 1896), pp. xxx-xlvii. Charles was of the opinion that Paul believed in seven heavens. The index entry "Heavens" in *OTP*, 2: 959-60 provides a convenient breakdown of each numbered level, and where it is mentioned in a given text. The best recent study is Bietenhard, *Die himmlische Welt*, pp. 3-18.

8. See Charlesworth's very handy summary of the major texts and how they describe and locate Paradise, *OTP*, 1: xxxiii. There is also the analysis of Joachim Jeremias, *TDNT*, s.v. "*paradeisos*, 5: 765-73.

9. For Luke it is likely below, in the Hadean world, see Luke 16:19-31 for his view of the place of the dead.

10. Scholem, *Jewish Gnosticism*, pp. 14-19; Bousset, "Himmelsreise der Seele," pp. 145-57; Bowker, "Merkabah Visions and Paul," pp. 157-73.

11. See Halperin, *The Merkabah in Rabbinic Literature*, pp. 86-92, for a full discussion and secondary literature. Urbach, predictably, opts for a metaphorical meaning. Henry A. Fischel has put together an impressive collection of evidence, arguing that the story was originally an anti-Epicurean parody, see his *Rabbinic Literature and Greco-Roman Philosophy* (Leiden: E. J. Brill, 1973), pp. 1-34. See Neusner's review of Fischel, now reprinted in *Ancient Judaism: Debates and Disputes*, pp. 73-75.

12. See the very helpful study by Morton Smith, "Transformation by Burial." Neither Phil. 1:23 nor 2 Cor. 5:6-10 place the dead in heaven before the parousia. The first refers to Paul's own special case, the second to the day of judgment.

13. See Dibelius, *Die Geisterwelt*; Bietenhard, *Die himmlische Welt*, pp. 101-42; G. B. Caird, *Principalities and Powers* (Oxford: Clarendon Press, 1956); and John J. Gunther, *Paul's Opponents*, pp. 172-208.

14. See Bo Reicke, "The Law and this World according to Paul," *JBL* 70 (1951): 259-76; G. H. C. MacGregor, "Principalities and Powers: The Cosmic

Background of Paul's Thought," *NTS* 1 (1954): 17-28.

15. On this material see Halperin, *The Merkabah in Rabbinic Literature*, pp. 107-140.

16.
This rather free translation of *embateuein*, as referring to a heavenly vision, was suggested by Bousset. See the essay by Francis, "Humility and Angelic Worship in Col. 2:18" and "The Background of *Embateuein* (Col. 2:18) in Legal Papyri and Oracle Inscriptions," in *Conflict at Colossae*, ed. and trans. Fred O. Francis and Wayne A. Meeks (Missoula: Scholars Press, 1975), pp. 163-95, 197-207.

17. See Lincoln, "Paul the Visionary," p. 215. Schmithals, *Gnosticism*, pp. 209-18 sees this dispute over "in" or "out" of the body as a crucial part of Paul's debate with Gnostics.

18. See Windisch, *Der Zweite Korintherbrief*, pp. 374-76 on the various types of heavenly travel.

19. Bauer, *Lexicon*, 2d ed, p. 109.

20. *The Worse Attacks the Better* 175, cf. Euripides, *Bacchae* 472; *PGM* 3. 205.

21. See the references in Windisch, *Der Zweite Korintherbrief*, pp. 377-78.

22. See Pearson, *The Pneumatikos-Psychikos Terminology*, pp. 27-43.

23. See Mark 13:14. Our best evidence for this "silent" period, after Paul's death, but before 70 C.E., might well be 2 Thessalonians. The concern there with apocalyptic signs of the Day of the Lord (2:2), but especially the reference to the evil one who would "sit in the Temple of God, proclaiming himself to be God" (2:4), seems to be an explicit attempt to interpret Daniel 11 and 12 in the critical days before or during the war with Rome. Since this letter appears to come before 70 C.E. (and likely before the other deutero-Pauline letters) it might well reflect the speculations and expectations of Paul himself. It is later than Paul, but not that late.

24. This is what Paul calls Israel's "full inclusion" (Rom. 11:12).

25. See in particular Neusner's summary treatment of this crucial period in his chapter titled "The Mishnah In Context: Ways Not Taken," *Judaism: The Evidence of the Mishnah* (Chicago: University of Chicago Press, 1981), pp. 25-44.

ABBREVIATIONS

The following abbreviations are used in the notes and bibliography:

AJA	*American Journal of Archaeology*
ANET	*Ancient Near Eastern Texts Relating to the Old Testament*, ed. J. B. Pritchard
ANRW	*Aufstieg und Niedergang der Römischen Welt*, ed. Hildegard Temporini and Wolfgang Haase
APOT	*Apocrypha and Pseudepigrapha of the Old Testament*, ed. R. H. Charles
ARW	*Archiv für Religionswissenschaft*
BARB	*Bulletin de l'Académie Royale de Belgique*
BJRL	*Bulletin of the John Rylands Library*
CH	*Church History*
CBQ	*Catholic Biblical Quarterly*
HR	*History of Religions*
HTR	*Harvard Theological Review*
IDB	*Interpreter's Dictionary of the Bible*
JBL	*Journal of Biblical Literature*
JSNT	*Journal for the Study of the New Testament*
JSJ	*Journal for the Study of Judaism in the Persian, Hellenistic, and Roman Period*
JSS	*Journal of Semetic Studies*
JTC	*Journal for Theology and the Church*
LCL	*Loeb Classical Library*

NovT	*Novum Testamentum*
NTA	*New Testament Apocrypha*, ed. W. Schneemelcher and Edgar Hennecke
NTS	*New Testament Studies*
OCD	*Oxford Classical Dictionary*, 2d ed.
OTP	*Old Testament Pseudepigrapha*, ed. J. H. Charlesworth
RB	*Revue Biblique*
RGG	*Die Religion in Geschichte und Gegenwart*, 3d ed.
RhM	*Rheinisches Museum für Philologie, Neue Folge*
RSR	*Recherches de Science Religieuse*
RQ	*Restoration Quarterly*
Str-B	*Kommentar zum Neuen Testament*, ed. H. Strack and P. Billerbeck
TDNT	*Theological Dictionary of the New Testament*, ed. G. Kittel and G. Friedrich
TZ	*Tübinger Zeitschrift*
VT	*Vetus Testamentum*
ZAW	*Zeitschrift für die altestamenliche Wissenschaft*

BIBLIOGRAPHY

The following works are cited in the text or notes:

Adam, James, ed. *The Republic of Plato.* 2 vols. Cambridge: University Press, 1929.

Anrich, Gustav. *Das antike Mysterienwesen in seinem Einfluss auf das Christentum.* Göttingen: n.p., 1894.

Aune, David. "The Problem of the Genre of the Gospels: A Critique of C. H. Talbert's What is a Gospel?" In *Gospel Perspectives: Studies of History and Tradition in the Four Gospels,* 1: 20-34. Edited by R. T. France and David Wenham. 2 vols. Sheffield: JSOT, 1981.

Baird, William. "Visions, Revelations, and Ministry." *JBL* 104 (1985): 651-62.

Barrett, C. K. *From First Adam to Last: A Study in Pauline Theology.* New York: Charles Scribner's Sons, 1962.

_____. "Paul's Opponents in II Corinthians." *NTS* 17 (1971): 233-54.

_____. *The Second Epistle to the Corinthians.* Harper's New Testament Commentaries. New York: Harper & Row, 1973.

Baur, F. C. "Die Christuspartei in der Korinthischen Gemeinde." *TZ* 4 (1831): 61-82

Beker, Christian J. *Paul's Apocalyptic Gospel.* (Philadelphia: Fortress Press, 1982).

_____. *Paul the Apostle.* Philadelphia: Fortress Press, 1980).

Betz, Hans Dieter. *Der Apostle Paulus und die sokratische Tradition: Eine exegetical Untersuchung zu seiner "Apologie" 2 Korinther 10-13.* Beiträge zur historischen Theologie, vol. 45. Tübingen: J. C. B. Mohr, 1972.

_____. *Galatians.* Hermeneia Commentary. Philadelphia: Fortress Press, 1979.

_____ed. *The Greek Magical Papyri in Translation*. Vol. 1: *Texts*. Chicago: University of Chicago Press, 1986.

_____. "On the Problem of the Religio-Historical Understanding of Apocalypticism." *JTC* 6 (1969): 134-56.

Beyerlin, Walter. *Origins and History of the Oldest Sinaitic Tradition*. Oxford: Blackwells, 1961.

Bickermann, Elias. "Die römische Kaiserapotheose." *ARW* 27 (1929): 1-27.

Bieler, Ludwig. *THEIOS ANER: Das Bild des "Göttlichen Menschen" in Spätantike und Frühchristentum*. 2 vols. Vienna: Oskar Hofels, 1935-36; reprint ed. in one vol., Darmstadt: Wissenschaftliche Buchgesellschaft, 1976.

Bietenhard, Hans. *Die himmlische Welt im Urchristentum und Spätjudentum*. Wissenschaftliche Untersuchungen zum Neuen Testament, no. 2. Tubingen: J. C. B. Mohr, 1951.

Blumenthal, David, ed. *Understanding Jewish Mysticism*. New York: KTAV, 1978.

Bornkamm, Günther. "The History of the Origin of the So-called Second Letter to the Corinthians." *NTS* 8 (1961): 258-64.

_____. *Paul*. Translated by D. M. G. Stalker. New York: Harper & Row, 1971.

Bousset, Wilhelm. "Die Himmelsreise der Seele." *ARW* 4 (1901): 136-69, 229-73.

Bowker, John W. "'Merkabah Visions' and the Visions of Paul." *JSS* 16 (1971): 57-73.

Brandenburger, Egon. *Adam und Christus: Exegetisch-religionsreschichtliche Untersuchung zu Röm. 5, 12-21 (1 Cor. 15)*. Wissenschaftliche Monographien zum Alten und Neuen Testament, vol. 7. Neukirchen: Neukirchen Verlag, 1962.

Brandon, S. G. F. *The Judgement of the Dead*. New York: Charles Scribner's Sons, 1967.

Bultmann, Rudolf. *The Theology of the New Testament*. Translated by Kendrick Grobel. 2 vols. New York: Charles Scribner's Sons, 1951-55.

Burkert, Walter. "*GOES*: zum griechischen 'Shamanismus'." *RhM* 105 (1962): 36-55.

BIBLIOGRAPHY

_____. *Lore and Science in Ancient Pythagoreanism*. Translated by Edwin L. Minar. Cambridge: Harvard University Press, 1972.

Caird, G. B. *Principalities and Powers: A Study in Pauline Theology*. Oxford: Clarendon Press, 1956.

Carr, Wesley. *Angels and Principalities: The Background, Meaning and Development of the Pauline Phrase hai archai kai hai exousiai*. Society of New Testament Studies Monograph Series, 42. Cambridge: Cambridge Univeristy, 1981.

Cartlidge, David B. and Dungan, David L., eds. *Documents for the Study of the Gospels*. Philadelphia: Fortress Press, 1980.

Cavallin, H. C. C. *Life After Death: Paul's Argument for the Resurrection of the Dead in I Cor. 15: Part I: An Enquiry into the Jewish Background*. Coniectanea biblica, New Testament, vol. 7:1. Lund: GWK Gleerup, 1974.

Charles, R. H., ed. *The Apocrypha and Pseudepigrapha of the Old Testament*. 2 vols. Oxford: Clarendon Press, 1912-13.

_____. *The Book of the Secrets of Enoch*. Translated by W. R. Morfill. Ozford: Clarendon Press, 1896.

_____. *Eschatology: The Doctrine of a Future Life in Israel, Judaism and Christianity: A Critical History*. n.p., 1913; reprint ed., New York: Schocken, 1963.

Charlesworth, James H., ed. *Old Testament Pseudepigrapha*. 2 vols. Garden City: Doubleday & Company, 1983-85.

_____. *The Pseudepigrapha and Modern Research With a Supplement*. Septuagint and Cognate Studies 7. Missoula: Scholars Press, 1981.

Collins, John J. "Cosmos and Salvation: Jewish jWisdom and Apocalyptic in the Hellenistic Age." *HR* 17 (1977): 121-42.

_____. *The Apocalyptic Imagination*. New York: Crossroad, 1984.

Colpe, Carsten. "Die Himmelsreise der Seele als philosophie- und religionsreschichtliche Problem." In *Festschrift für Joseph Klein*, pp. 85-104. Edited by Erich Fries. Göttingen: Vandenhoeck & Ruprecht, 1967.

Conzelmann, Hans. *First Corinthians*. Hermenia Commentary. Philadelphia: Fortress Press, 1975.

THINGS UNUTTERABLE: PAUL'S ASCENT TO PARADISE

Coxon, A. H. "Parmenides." In *Oxford Classical Dictionary*. 2d ed.

Craigie, P. C. "Helel, Athar and Plaethon." *ZAW* 85 (1973): 223-25.

Cumont, Franz. *Afterlife in Roman Paganism*. New Haven: Yale Univeristy Press, 1923.

_____. *Astrology and Religion Among the Greeks and Romans*. New York: G. P. Putnam's Sons, 1912.

_____. "Le mysticism astral dans l'antiquité." *BARB* 58 (1909): 256-86.

_____. *Recherches sur le symbolisme funéraire des Romains*. Paris: 1942)

Daniélou, Jean. *Gospel Message and Hellenistic Culture*. Translated by John A. Baker. Philadelphia: Westminster Press, 1973.

_____. *The Theology of Jewish Christianity*. Translated by John A. Baker. Chicago: Henry Regnery, 1964.

_____. "Les Traditions secrètes des Apôtres." *Eranos* 31 (1962): 199-215.

W. D. Davies. *Paul and Rabbinic Judaism: Some Rabbinic Elements in Pauline Theology*. 3d. ed. London: S.P.C.K., 1970.

Dean-Otting, Mary. *Heavenly Journeys: A Study of the Motif in Hellenistic Jewish Literature*. Judentum und Umwelt, no. 8. Frankfurt: P. Lang, 1984.

Deissmann, Adolf. *Bible Studies*. Edinburgh: T. & T. Clark, 1901.

_____. *Paul: A Study in Social and Religious History*. Translated by William E. Wilson. 2d ed. New York: Harper & Row, 1926.

Deissner, Kurt. *Paulus und die Mystik seiner Zeit*. 2d ed. Leipzig: A. Deichert'sche Verlagsbuchhandlung, 1921.

Denis, Albert M. *Fragmenta pseudepigraphorum quae supersunt Graeca*. Leiden: E. J. Brill, 1970.

Dibelius, Martin. *Die Geisterwelt im Glauben des Paulus*. Göttingen: Vandenhoeck & Ruprecht, 1909.

Dicks, D. R. *Early Greek Astronomy to Aristotle*. Ithaca: Cornell University Press, 1970.

BIBLIOGRAPHY

Diels, Hermann. *Die Fragmente der Vorsokratiker.* Edited by Walter Kranz. 10th ed. 3 vols. Berlin: Weidmann, 1960-61.

_____, ed. *Poetarum Philosophorum Fragmenta.* Berlin: Weidmann, 1901.

Dieterich, Albrecht. *Eine Mithrasliturgie.* 3d ed. Edited by Otto Weinreich. Leipzig: B. G. Teubner, 1923.

Dodd, C. H. *The Bible and the Greeks.* London: Hodder & Stoughton, 1935.

Dodds, E. R. *The Greeks and the Irrational.* Berkeley: Univeristy of California Press, 1971.

_____. E. R. *Pagan and Christian in an Age of Anxiety.* New York: W. W. Norton, 1965.

Dunn, James G. *Christology in the Making.* Philadelphia: Westminster, 1980.

_____. *Jesus and the Spirit.* Philadelphia: Westminster, 1975.

Ellis, E. Earle. "Paul and His Opponents." In *Christianity, Judaism, and Other Greco-Roman Cults, 2: 264-98.* Edited by Jacob Neusner. 4 vols. Leiden: E. J. Brill, 1975.

Eltester, Friedrich W. *Eikon im Neuen Testament.* Beihefte zur Zeitschrift für die neutestamentliche Wissenschaft, no. 23. Berlin: A. Töpelmann, 1958.

Enslin, M. *Reapproaching Paul.* Philadelphia: Westminster, 1972.

Farnell, Lewis R. *Greek Hero Cults and Ideas of Immortality.* Oxford: Clarendon Press, 1921.

Festugière, André-Jean. *Hermétisme et Mystique Paienne.* Paris: Aubier-Montaigne, 1967.

_____. *Personal Religion Among the Greeks.* Berkeley: Univeristy of California Press, 1960.

_____. *La revelation d'Hermès Trismégiste.* 4 vols. Paris: Gabalda, 1944-54.

Fiorenza, Elizabeth Schüssler. *In Memory of Her: A Feminist Reconstruction of Christian Origins.* New York: Crossroad: 1983.

Fischel, Henry A. *Rabbinic Literature and Greco-Roman Philosophy*. Leiden: E. J. Brill, 1973.

Francis, Fred, and Wayne A. Meeks, eds. *Conflict at Colossae*. Sources for Biblical Study, no. 4. Missoula: Scholars Press, 1974.

Friedrich, Gerhard. "Die Gegner des Paulus im zweiten Korintherbrief." In *Abraham Unser Vater*, pp. 181-215. Edited by Otto Betz, Martin Hengel and Peter Schmidt. Leiden: E. J. Brill, 1963.

Gallagher, Eugene V. *Divine Man or Magician?: Celsus and Origen on Jesus*. SBL Dissertation Series, no. 64. Missoula: Scholars Press, 1982.

Gaster, T. H. "Cosmogony." In *Interpreter's Dictionary of the Bible*, 1:702-8.

Georgi, Dieter. *Die Gegner des Paulus im 2 Korintherbrief: Studien zur religiösen Propaganda in der Spätantike*. Wissenschaftliche Monographien zum Alten und Neuen Testament, vol. 11. Neukirchen-Vluyn: Neukirchener Verlag, 1964.

_____. *Die Geschichte der Kollekte des Paulus für Jerusalem*. Hamburg: Herbert Reich Verlag, 1965.

Glasson, T. Francis. *Greek Influence in Jewish Eschatology*. London: S.P.C.K., 1961.

Goodenough, E. R. *Jewish Symbols in the Greco-Roman Period*. 11 vols. New York: Pantheon Books, 1953-1964.

Grant, R. M. *Augustus to Constantine*. New York: Harper and Row, 1970.

_____. "Early Alexandrian Christianity." *CH* 40 (1971): 133-44.

_____. *Gnosticism and Early Christianity*. New York: Columbia University Press, 1959, reprinted with revisions and a new chapter, Harper Torchbook edition, New York: Harper & Row, 1966.

_____. "Jewish Christianity at Antioch in the Second Century." *RSR* 60 (1972): 97-108.

Gressmann, Hugo. *Die hellenistische Gestirnreligion*. Beihefte zum Altern Orient, no. 5. Leipzig: Hinrich, 1925.

Griffiths, J. Gwyn. *The Isis-Book*. Etudes Préliminaires aux Religions Orientales dans L'Empire Romain, vol. 39. Leiden: E. J. Brill, 1975.

BIBLIOGRAPHY

Gruenwald, Ithamar. *Apocalyptic and Merkavah Mysticism.* Arbeiten zur Geschichte des antiken Judentums und des Urchristentums, vol. 14. Leiden: E. J. Brill, 1980.

Grundy, Robert H. *Soma in Biblical Theology with Emphasis on Pauline Anthropology.* Society for New Testament Studies Monography Series, no. 29. Cambridge: University Press, 1976.

Gunkel, Hermann. *Schöpfung und Chaos in Urzeit und Endzeit.* Göttingen: Vandenhoeck & Ruprecht, 1895.

Gunther, John J. *St. Paul's Opponents and Their Background: A Study of Apocalyptic and Jewish Sectarian Teachings.* Supplements Novum Testamentum, vol. 35. Leiden: E. J. Brill, 1973.

Guthrie, W. C. K.*The Greeks and Their Gods.* Boston: Beacon Press, 1950.

Güttgemanns, Erhardt. *Der leidende Apostel und sein Herr: Studien zur paulinischen Christologie.* Forschungen zur Religion und Literatur des Alten und Neuen Testaments, vol. 90. Göttingen: Vandennhoeck & Ruprecht, 1966.

Halperin, David J. *The Merkabah in Rabbinic Literature.* American Oriental Series, vol. 62. New Haven: American Oriental Society, 1980.

Heidel, Alexander.*The Babylonians Genesis.* Chicago: University of Chicago Press, Pheonix Books, 1963.

_____. *The Gilgamesh Epic and Old Testament Parallels.* Chicago: University of Chicago Press, Phoenix Books, 1963.

Hennecke, Edgar. *New Testament Apocrypha.* Edited by Wilhelm Schneemelcher and translated by R. McL. Wilson. 2 vols. Philadelphia: Westminster Press, 1965.

Holladay, Carl. *Theios Anēr in Hellenistic Judaism.* SBL Dissertation Series, 40. Missoula: Scholar's Press, 1977.

Holmberg, Bengt. *Paul and Power: The Structure of Authority in the Primitive Church as Reflected in the Pauline Epistles.* Philadelphia: Fortress Press, 1978.

Jacobsen, Thorkild. "Mesopotamia." In *Before Philosophy,* pp. 137-234. Edited by J. A. Frankfort. Baltimore: Penguin Books, 1946.

_____. *The Sumerian King List.* Assyrian Studies, no. 6. Chicago: University of Chicago Press.

THINGS UNUTTERABLE: PAUL'S ASCENT TO PARADISE

Jaeger, Werner. "The Greek Ideas of Immortality." In *Immortality and Resurrection: Death in the Western World: Two Conflicting Currents of Thought*, pp. 97-114. Edited by Krister Stendahl. New York: Macmillan, Macmillan Paperback, 1965.

Jervell, Jacob. *Imago Dei, Gen. 1:26f im Spätjudentum, in der Gnosis und in den paulinischen Briefen*. Forschungen zur Religion und Literatur des Alten und Neuen Testaments, vol. 76. Göttingen: Vandenhoeck & Ruprecht, 1960.

Jewett, Robert. *A Chronology of Paul's Life*. Philadelphia: Fortress Press, 1979.

——————————. *Paul's Anthropological Terms: A Study of their Use in Conflict Settings*. Arbeiten zur Geschichte des antiken Judentums und des Urchristentums, vol. 10. Leiden: E. J. Brill, 1971.

Käsemann, Ernst. *Commentary on Romans*. Translated and edited by Geoffrey W. Bromiley. Grand Rapids: William B. Eerdmans, 1980.

——————————. "Justification and Salvation History." In *Perspectives on Paul*, pp. 60-78. Translated by Margret Kohl. Philadelphia: Fortress Press, 1971.

Kennedy, H. A. A. *St. Paul and the Mystery Religions*. London: Hodder & Stoughton, 1913

Knox, John. *Chapters in a Life of Paul*. Nashville: Abingdon Press, 1950.

Koester, Helmut. "Gnomai Diaphoroi." *HTR* 58 (1965): 279-318.

Kramer, S. N. *Sumerian Mythology*. Philadelphia: American Philosophical Society, 1944.

Lattimore, Richard. *Themes in Greek and Latin Epitaphs*. Urbana: University of Illinois Press, 1942.

Lietzmann, Hans. *An die Korinther I-II*. Edited by W. G. Kümmel. Handbuch zum Neuen Testament, no. 9. 4th ed. Tübingen: J. C. B. Mohr, 1949.

Lincoln, A. T. *Paradise Now and Not Yet: Studies in the Role of the Heavenly Dimension in Paul's Thought with Special Reference to his Eschatology*. Society of New Testament Studies Monograph Series, 43. Cambridge: Cambridge University Press, 1981.

——————————. "'Paul the Visionary': The Setting and Significance of the Rapture to Paradise in II Corinthians XII. 1-10." *NTS* 25 (1978): 204-20.

BIBLIOGRAPHY

Lohfink, Gerhard. *Die Himmelfahrt Jesus.* Studien zum Alten und Neuen Testament, vol. 26. Munich: Kosel Verlag, 1971.

Luck, Georg. "Studia divina in vita humana: On Cicero's 'Dream of Scipio' and its Place in Graeco-Roman Philosophy." *HTR* 49 (1956): 207-18.

Luedemann, Gerd. *Paul Apostle to the Gentiles: Studies in Chronology.* Philadelphia: Fortress Press, 1984.

Macgregor, G. H. C. "Principalities and Powers: The Cosmic Background of Paul's Thought." *NTS* 1 (1954): 541-64.

McKay, J. W. "Helel and the Dawn-Goddess: A Reexamination of the Myth in Isaiah 12-15." *VT* 20 (1970): 541-64.

Maier, Johann. "Das Gefahrdungsmotiv bei der Himmelsreise in der Judischen Apocalyptik und Gnosis." *Kairos* 5 (1963): 18-40.

Martin, Ralph P. *Carmen Christi: Philippians ii. 5-11 in Recent Interpretation and in the Setting of Early Christian Worship.* 2d ed. Grand Rapids: Eerdmans, 1983.

Meeks, Wayne. "Moses as God and King." In *Religions in Antiquity*, pp. 354-71. Edited by Jacob Neusner. Studies in the History of Religions, vol. 14. Leiden: E. J. Brill;, 1968.

_____. *The Prophet King.* Leiden: E. J. Brill, 1967.

_____. *The Writings of St. Paul.* Norton Critical Edition. New York: W. W. Norton, 1972.

Metzger, Bruce. *Index to Periodical Literature on the Apostle Paul.* New York: United Bible Societies, 1971.

Meyer, Marvin, ed. and trans. *The "Mithras Liturgy."* Texts and Translations 10: Graeco-Roman Religion Series, 2. Missoula: Scholars Press, 1976.

Meyer, Richard. "Mimmelfahrt." In *RGG*, 3: 333-35.

Milik, J. T. *The Books of Enoch: Aramaic Fragments of Qumran Cave 4.* Oxford: Clarendon Press, 1976.

Moran, William L., ed. *Toward the Image of Tammuz.* Cambridge: Harvard University Press, 1970.

Munck, Johannes. *Christ and Israel: An Interpretation of Romans 9-11.* Translated by Ingeborg Nixon. Philadelphia: Fortress Press, 1967.

Munck_____. *Paul and the Salvation of Mankind.* Translated by Frank Clarke. Richmond: John Knox Press, 1959.

Murphy-O'Conner, J. "Christological Anthropology in Phil. 2:6-11." *RB* 83 (1976): 25-50.

Neusner, Jacob. *Ancient Judaism: Debates and Disputes.* Brown Judaic Studies, no. 64. Chico: Scholars Press, 1984.

_____. Review of Joseph Bonsirven, *Palestinian Judaism in the Time of Jesus Christ* Robert M. Grant, *Gnosticism in Early Christianity* (rev. ed. 1966) in *Judaism* 15 (1966): 230-40. Reprinted in Jacob Neusner, *Ancient Judaism: Debates and Disputes*, pp. 79-89.

_____. "Comparing Judaisms: Essay-Review of *Paul and Pales tinian Judaism* by E. P. Sanders." *HR* 18 (1978): 177-91. Reprinted in *Ancient Judaism: Debates and Disputes*, pp. 127-141.

_____, ed. *Christianity, Judaism, and Other Greco-Roman Cults: Studies for Morton Smith at Sixty.* 4 vols. Leiden: E. J. Brill, 1975.

_____. *Development of a Legend: Studies in the Traditions Concerning Yohanan ben Zakkai.* Leiden: E. J. Brill, 1970.

_____. "The Development of the Merkavah Tradition." *JSJ* 2 (1971): 149-60.

_____. *Judaism: The Development of the Mishnah.* Chicago: University of Chicago Press, 1981.

_____. *A Life of Yohanan ben Zakkai.* Leiden: E. J. Brill, 1970.

_____, ed. *Religions in Antiquity: Essays in Memory of Erwin Ramsdell Goodenough.* Leiden: E. J. Brill, 1968.

Neyrey, Jerome H. "The Form and Background of the Polemic in 2 Peter." *JBL* 99 (1980): 4078-31.

Nickelsburg, George W. E., Jr. *Resurrection, Immortality and Eternal Life in Intertestamental Judaism.* Harvard Theological Studies, vol. 26. Cambridge: Harvard University Press, 1972.

Nickle, Keith F. *The Collection: A Study in Paul's Strategy.* Studies in Biblical Theology, no. 48. Naperville, IL: Allenson, 1966.

Niditch, S. "The Visionary." In *Ideal Figures in Ancient Judaism*, pp. 153-79. Edited by G. W. E. Nickelsburg and J. J. Collins. Missoula: Scholars Press, 1980.

BIBLIOGRAPHY

Nilsson, Martin. "Die astrale Unsterblichkeit und der kosmische Mystik." *Numen* 1 (1954): 106-19.

_____. *Geschichte der griechischen Religion.* Handbuch der Alter tumswissenschaft, vol. 5:2. 2 vols. Munich: Beck, 1967.

_____. *Greek Piety.* Translated by J. J. Rose. New York: W. W. Norton, 1969.

_____. "History of Greek Religion in the Hellenistic and Roman Age." *HTR* 36 (1943): 251-75.

_____. "The New Conception of the Universe in Late Greek Paganism." *Eranos* 44 (1946): 20-27.

Nock, Arthur Darby. *Conversion: The Old and the New in Religions from Alexander the Great to Augustine of Hippo.* Oxford: Oxford University Press, Oxford Paperbacks, 1961.

_____. "The Cult of Heroes." *HTR* 37 (1944): 141-74.

_____. *Early Gentile Christianity and Its Hellenistic Background.* New York: Harper & Row, 1964.

_____. *Essays on Religion and the Ancient World.* Edited by Zeph Stewart. 2 Vols. Cambridge: Harvard University Press, 1972.

_____. ed. and Festugière, A.-J. trans. *Hermès Trismégiste.* 3d ed. 4 vols. Paris: Société d'Edition les Belles Lettres, 1946-54.

_____. "Sarcophagi and Symbolism." *AJA* 50 (1946): 140-70.

_____. "A Vision of Mandulis Aion." *HTR* 27 (1934): 53-104.

Oostendorp, D. W. *Another Jesus: A Gospel of Jewish-Christian Superiority in II Corinthians.* Kampen: J. J. Kok, 1967.

Oppenheim, A. Leo. "The Interpretation of Dreams in the Ancient Near East." *APS* 46 (1956): 259-87.

Pearson, Birger A. *The Pneumatikos-Psychikos Terminology.* SBL Dissertation Series, no. 12. Missoula: Scholars Press, 1973.

Pellikann-Engel, Maja E. *Hesiod and Parmenides: A New View on their Cosmologies and on Parmenides' Proem.* Amsterdam: Adolf M. Hakkert, 1974.

141

Plummer, Alfred. *Second Epistle of St. Paul to the Corinthians.* International Critical Commentary. Edinburgh: T & T. Clark, 1915.

Preisendanz, Karl, ed. *Papyri Graecae Magicae.* 2d ed. edited by Albert Henrichs. 2 vols. Stuttgart: B. G. Teubner, 1973-74.

Price, Robert. "Punished in Paradise (An Exegetical Theory of II Corinthians 12:1-10)." *JSNT* 7 (1980): 33-40.

Pritchard, James B., ed. *The Ancient Near East Relating to the Old Testament.* 2d ed. Princeton: Princeton University Press, 1955.

Reike, Bo. "The Law and the Elements of the World According to Paul." Translated by William B. Schaeffer. *JBL* 70 (1951): 259-76.

Reitzenstein, Richard. *Hellenistic Mystery-Religions: Their Basic Ideas and Significance.* Translated by John E. Steely. Pittsburgh Theological Monograph Series, no. 15. Pittsburgh: Pickwick Press, 1978.

_____. *Hellenistische Wundererzählungen.* 2d ed. Leipzig: B. G. Teubner, 1922; reprint ed., Stuttgart: B. G. Teubner, 1963.

_____. *Poimandres: Studien zum griechisch-ägyptischen und frühchristlichen Literatur.* Leipzig: B. G. Teubner, 1904; reprint ed., Stuttgard: B. G. Teubner, 1966.

Robertson, Archibald and Alfred Plummer. *First Epistle of St. Paul to the Corinthians.* International Critical Commentary. 2d ed. Edinburgh: T & T. Clark, 1914.

Robinson, James M., ed. *The Nag Hammadi Library.* New York: Harper & Row, 1977.

Rohde, Erwin. *Psyche: The Cult of Souls and Belief in Immortality Among the Greeks.* Translated by W. B. Hillis. 8th ed. New York: Harcourt, Brace & Co., 1925.

Roloff, D. *Göttahnlichkeit, Vergöttlichung und Erhöhung zu Seligem Leben: Untersuchungen zur Herkunft der platonischen Angleichung an Gott.* Berlin: W. de Gruyter, 1970.

Rudolf, Kurt. *Gnosis: The Nature and History of Gnosticism.* Translated by Robert McLachlan Wilson. San Francisco: Harper & Row, 1985.

Russell, D. S. *The Method and Message of Jewish Apocalyptic.* Philadelphia: Westminster Press, 1964.

BIBLIOGRAPHY

Saake, Helmut. "Paulus als Ekstatiker: Pneumatologische Beobachtungen zu 2 Kor. xiii. 1-10." *NovT* 15 (1973): 153-60.

Sanders, E. P. *Paul and Palestinian Judaism: A Comparison of Patterns of Religion.* Philadelphia: Fortress Press, 1977.

_____. *Paul, the Law, and the Jewish People.* Philadelphia: Fortress Press, 1983.

Sandmel, Samuel. "Parallelomania." *JBL* 81 (1962): 1-13.

Sass, Gerhard. *Apostelamt und Kirche: Eine theologisch- exegetische Unter suchung des paulinischen Apostelbegriffs.* Forschung zur Geschichte und Lehre des Protestantismus, vol. 9:2. Munich: C. Kaiser, 1939.

Schmithals, Walter. *Gnosticism in Corinth: An Investigation of the Letters to the Corinthians.* Translated by John E. Steely. Nashville: Abingdon Press, 1971.

Schoeps, Hans J. *Paul: The Theology of the Apostle in the Light of Jewish Religious History.* Translated by Harold Knight. Philadelphia: Westminster Press, 1959.

Scholem, Gershom. *Jewish Gnosticism, Merkabah Mysticism and the Talmudic Tradition.* 2d ed. New York: Jewish Theological Seminary of America, 1960.

Schütz, John Howard. *Paul and the Anatomy of Apostolic Authority.* Society for New Testament Studies Monograph Series, no. 26. Cambridge: University Press, 1975.

Schweitzer, Albert. *The Mysticism of Paul the Apostle.* Translated by William Montgomery. London: Adam & Charles Black, 1953.

Scott, Walter and A. S. Ferguson, eds. *Hermetica.* 4 vols. Oxford: Clarendon Press, 1924-26.

Scroggs, Robin. *The Last Adam: A Study in Pauline Anthropology.* Philadelphia: Fortress Press, 1966.

Segal, Alan F. "Heavenly Ascent in Hellenistic Judaism, Early christianity and their Environment." In *Aufstieg und Niedergang der Römischen Welt, Principat II,* 23 (1980): 1333-94. Edited by Wolfgang Haase. Berlin: Walter de Gruyter, 1972-

Smith, Jonathan Z. "Good News is No News." In *Map is Not Territory,* pp. 190-207. Studies in Judaism in Late Antiquity, vol. 23. Leiden: E. J. Brill, 1978.

_____. "Hellenistic Religions." In *The New Encyclopedia Britannica, Macropaedia*, 8: 749-51. 15th. ed.

_____. "Native Cults in the Hellenistic Period." *HR* 11 (1971): 236-249.

_____. Review of *Le origini dello gnosticismo*, edited by Ugo Bianchi. *Kairos* 10 (1968): 298-302.

_____. "The Prayer of Joseph." In *Map is Not Territory*, pp. 24-66. Studies in Judaism in Late Antiquity, vol. 23. Leiden: E. J. Brill, 1978.

_____. "Wisdom and Apocalyptic." In *Religious Syncretism in Antiquity: Essays in Conversation with Geo Widengren*, pp. 131-56. Edited by Birger A. Pearson. Missoula: Scholars Press, 1975.

Smith, Morton. *Clement of Alexandria and a Secret Gospel of Mark*. Cambridge: Harvard University Press, 1973.

_____. "The Common Theology of the Ancient Near East." *JBL* 71 (1952): 135-47.

_____. "Goodenough's *Jewish Symbols* in Retrospect." *JBL* 86 (1967): 53-68.

_____. "The Image of God: Notes on the Hellenization of Judaism, with Especial Reference to Goodenough's Work on Jewish Symbols." *BJRL* 40 (1958): 473-512.

_____. *Jesus the Magician*. New York: Harper & Row, 1978.

_____. "Observations on Hekhalot Rabbati." in *Biblical and Other Studies*, pp. 142-160. Edited by Alexander Altmann. Cambridge: Harvard University Press, 1963.

_____. "On the History of the Divine Man." in *Paganisme, Judaïsme, Christianisme* (Marcel Simon Festschrift), pp. 335-45. Edited by André Benoit, Marc Philonenko and Cyrille Vogel. Paris: É. de Boccard, 1978.

_____. "Prolegomena to a Discussion of Aretologies, Divine Men, the Gospels and Jesus." *JBL* 90 (1971): 174-99.

_____. "Salvation in the Gospels, Paul, and the Magical Papyri." *Helios* 13 (1986): 63-74.

BIBLIOGRAPHY

_____. "Transformation by Burial." *Eranos* 52 (1983): 87-112.

Spittler, Russell. "The Limits of Ecstasy: An Exegesis of 2 Corinthians 12:1-10." In *Current Issues in Biblical and Patristic Interpretation*, pp. 259-66. Edited by Gerald F. Hawthorne. Grand Rapids: William B. Eerdmans, 1975.

Spörlein, Bernhard. *Die Leugnung der Auferstehung.* Biblische Untersuchungen, vol. 7. Regensburg: Verlag Friedrich Pustet, 1971.

Stanley, D. M. "The Theme of the Servant of Yahweh in Primitive Christian Soteriology and its Transformation by St. Paul." *CBQ* 16 (1954): 385-425.

Stendahl, Krister. "The Apostle Paul and the Introspective Conscience of the West." *HTR* 56 (1963): 199-215.

Stone, Michael. "Apocalyptic--Vision or Hallucination." *Milla wa-Milla* 14 (1974): 47-56.

_____. "Lists of Revealed Things in the Apocalyptic Literature." In *Magnalia Dei: The Mighty Acts of God.*, pp. 439-43. Edited by F. M. Cross, W. E. Lemke, and P. D. Miller, Jr. Garden City: Doubleday, 1976.

_____. *Scriptures, Sects and Visions.* Philadelphia: Fortress Press, 1976.

Strugnell, John. "The Angelic Liturgy at Qumrân--4Q Serek Šîrôt 'Ôlat Haśśabbat." *Vetus Testamentum Supplment* 7 (1960): 318-345.

Suter, David W. *Tradition and Composition in the Parables of Enoch.* SBL Dissertation Series, no. 47. Missoula: Scholars Press, 1979.

Tabor, James D. "Paul's Notion of Many 'Sons of God' and its Hellenistic Contexts. *Helios* 13 (1986): 87-97.

_____. "Resurrection and Immortality: Paul and Poimandres." In *Christian Teaching: Studies in Honor of LeMoine G. Lewis*, pp. 72-91. Edited by Everett Ferguson. Abilene: Abilene Christian University Press, 1981.

_____. "The Theology of Redemption in Theophilus of Antioch." *Restoration Quarterly* 18 (1975): 159-71.

Talbert, Charles. "The Problem of Pre-existence in Phil. 2:6-11," *JBL* 86 (1967): 141-153.

145

Taran, Leonard, ed. *Parmenides: A Text with Translation, Commentary, and a Critical Essay.* Princeton: Princeton University Press, 1965.

Wagner, Günther. *Pauline Baptism and the Pagan Mysteries.* Translated by J. P. Smith. Edinburgh: Oliver & Boyd, 1967.

Walton, Francis R. s.v. "Afterlife." *Oxford Classical Dictionary.* 2d ed.

Wertmeimer, Solomon, ed. *Batte Midrashot.* 2 vols. Jerusalem: Mossad Karov Kook, 1968.

Widengren, Geo. *The Ascension of the Apostle and the Heavenly Book.* Uppsala Universitets Årsskrift, no. 7. Uppsala: A. B. Lundequistska, 1950.

Wilcke, H.-A. *Das Problem eines messianischen Zwischenreiches bei Paulus.* Abhandlungen zur Theologie des Alten und Neuen Testament, vol. 51. Zurich: Zwingli Verlag, 1967.

Wilckens, Ulrich. *Weisheit und Torheit: Eine exegetisch- religionsgeschichtliche Untersuchung zu I Kor. 1 und 2.* Beiträge zur historischen Theologie, vol. 26. Tübingen: J. C. B. Mohr, 1959.

Wilken, Robert L. *The Myth of Christian Beginnings.* Notre Dame: University of Notre Dame Press, reprint of the 1971 ed., 1980.

Wilkenhauser, Alfred. *Pauline Mysticism.* Translated by Joseph Cunningham. New York: Herder & Herder, 1960.

Windisch, Hans. *Paulus und Christus: Ein biblisch- religionsgeschichtliches Vergleich.* Untersuchungen zum Neuen Testament, vol 24. Leipzig: J. C. Hinrichs, 1934.

_____. *Der Zweite Korintherbrief.* 9th ed. Gottingen: Vandenhoeck & Ruprecht, 1924.

Woll, Bruce. "The Departure of 'The Way': The First Farewell Discourse in the Gospel of John," *JBL* 99 (1980): 225-39.

Zmijewski, Josef. *Der Stil der paulinischen "Narrenrede": Analyse der Sprach gestaltung in 2 Kor 11, 1-12,10.* Bonner biblische Beiträge, no. 12. Cologne: Peter Hanstein Verlag, 1978.

INDEX OF ANCIENT NAMES AND SOURCES

The following are cited in the text or notes. Page numbers are listed, with note reference numbers in parentheses. References to the Hebrew Bible, the New Testament and the Apocrypha are not included.

INDEX OF MODERN AUTHORS

INDEX

151

GENERAL SUBJECT INDEX

About the Author

James D. Tabor teaches Christian origins in the Religion Department at the college of William and Mary. He has degrees from Abilene Christian University, Pepperdine University, and the University of Chicago. His research focuses on ways of understanding "salvation" in ancient Mediterranean religions, including early Christianity and forms of Second Temple Judaism.